Starting Up an Online Business

PEARSON

Harlow, England • London • New York • Boston • San Francisco • Toronto • Sydney • Auckland • Singapore • Hong Kong
Tokyo • Seoul • Taipei • New Delhi • Cape Town • São Paulo • Mexico City • Madrid • Amsterdam • Munich • Paris • Milan

PEARSON EDUCATION LIMITED
Edinburgh Gate
Harlow CM20 2JE
United Kingdom
Tel: +44 (0)1279 623623
Web: www.pearson.com/uk

First published 2013 (print and electronic)

ISBN: 978-0-273-77474-7 (print)
         978-0-273-77588-1 (PDF)

British Library Cataloguing-in-Publication Data
A catalogue record for the print edition is available from the British Library

Library of Congress Cataloging-in-Publication Data
A catalog record for the print edition is available from the Library of Congress

Microsoft screenshots in this book are reprinted by permission of Microsoft
Corporation.

Contains public sector information licensed under the Open Government Licence
(OGL) v1.0. www.nationalarchives.gov.uk/doc/open-government-licence.

10 9 8 7 6 5 4 3 2 1
16 15 14 13

Print edition typeset in 11/14pt ITC Stone Sans by 3
Print edition printed and bound in Great Britain by Ashford Colour Press Ltd, Gosport, Hampshire

NOTE THAT ANY PAGE CROSS REFERENCES REFER TO THE PRINT EDITION

Starting Up an Online Business

in Simple steps

Heather Morris

Starting up an online business with confidence

Get to grips with practical computing tasks with minimal time, fuss and bother. *In Simple Steps* guides guarantee immediate results. They tell you everything you need to know on a specific application from the most essential tasks to master to every activity you'll want to accomplish, through to solving the most common problems you'll encounter.

Helpful features

To build your confidence and help you start up an online business, practical hints, tips and shortcuts feature on every page:

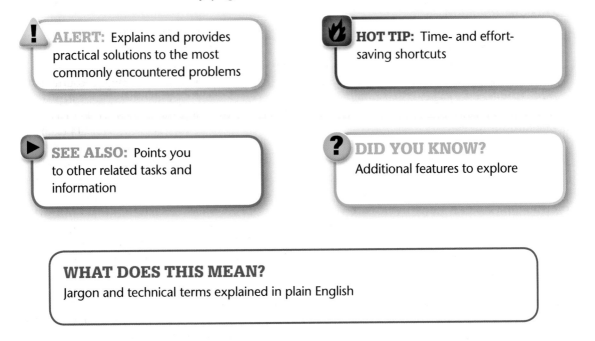

ALERT: Explains and provides practical solutions to the most commonly encountered problems

HOT TIP: Time- and effort-saving shortcuts

SEE ALSO: Points you to other related tasks and information

DID YOU KNOW? Additional features to explore

WHAT DOES THIS MEAN? Jargon and technical terms explained in plain English

Practical. Simple. Fast.

in Simple steps

Dedication

For Finley and Callum.

Acknowledgements

I would like to thank the publishing team who helped create this book, including Steve Temblett, Rob Cottee, Sundus Pasha and Viv Church. I'm grateful to be an author in this excellent series. I'd also like to thank Neil Salkind for his encouragement and for continuing to help me find such interesting projects.

Publisher acknowledgements

We are grateful to the following for permission to reproduce copyright material:

Screenshots

Pages 2, 3 (top), 3 (bottom), 8, 20, 21 (top), 21 (bottom), 96, 97, 98, 100, 101, 166, 167: Screenshots courtesy of Google; Page 14: Screenshot of ipo.gov.uk homepage, Intellectual Property Office, © Crown copyright; Page 17: Screenshot of www.sunfloweruk.com homepage, Courtesy of Sunflower Marketing, Design and Communications; Page 18: Screenshot of www.custommade-uk.co.uk hompage, courtesy of Custom M.A.D.E. Ltd; Page 22: Screenshot of www.startups.co.uk, courtesy of Crimson Publishing Ltd; Pages 26, 31, 32, 37, 110 (top), 110 (bottom), 111, 113, 114, 115, 162: Microsoft screenshots in this book are reprinted by permission of Microsoft Corporation; Pages 12, 27, 139, 140, 141, 142, 143, 144 (top), 144 (bottom), 145, 146, 147, 148, 149: Screenshots courtesy of Amazon UK; Page 33: Screenshot of www.domaincheck.co.uk purchase screen, courtesy of Domaincheck; Page 35: Screenshot of www.webhostdir.co.uk homepage; courtesy of Serchen Ltd; Page 51: Screenshot of www.hmrc.gov.uk/vat/index.htm VAT information screen, HM Revenue & Customs, © Crown copyright; Page 103: Screenshot of pinterest.com/ selected products screen, courtesy of Pinterest; Page 108: Screenshot of www.electronic-payments.co.uk compare online payment solutions screen, Courtesy of and copyright © RSTO Limited; Page 112: Screenshot of www.cnet.co.uk/ AVG Anti-Virus Free Edition 2012 1012.0.1913 download screen, copyright © The YGS group; Page 153: Screenshot of www.businesslink.gov.uk, homepage, © Crown copyright; Page 154: Screenshot of www.hmrc.gov.uk/startingup 'Starting in business' information screen, HM Revenue & Customs, © Crown copyright; Page 155: Screenshot of www.hmrc.gov.uk/sa/rec-keep-self-emp.htm 'Record keeping (self-employed) screen, HM Revenue & Customs, © Crown copyright; Page 157: Screenshot of oft.gov.uk homepage, Office of Fair Trading, © Crown copyright; Page 159: Screenshot of ipo.gov.uk/tm/t-find/t-find-text/ 'Trade Mark Enquiry' screen, Intellectual Property Office, © Crown copyright; Page 160: Screenshot of www.ipo.gov.uk/types/copy.htm copyright information screen, Intellectual Property Office, © Crown copyright; Page 172: Screenshot of www.financialfraudaction.org.uk/retailer-landing.asp 'Retailer landing page', courtesy of Financial Fraud Action UK.

In some instances we have been unable to trace the owners of copyright material, and we would appreciate any information that would enable us to do so.

in Simple
steps

Contents at a glance

Top 10 Online Start-up Problems Solved

Contents

Top 10 Online Start-up Tips

1 Develop your business idea

7 Explore other payment options and online security

8 Sell on eBay

9 Sell on Amazon

10 Understand tax and legal obligations

Top 10 Online Start-up Problems Solved

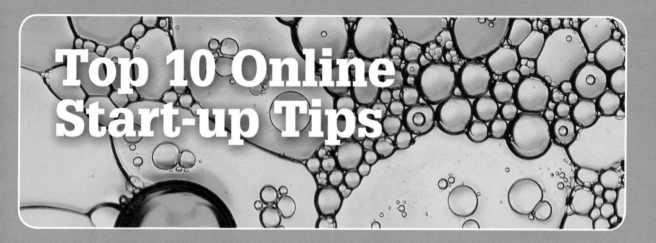

Top 10 Online Start-up Tips

Tip 1: Assess demand for your idea

You can find out how many people are searching the Internet for a specific item by looking at keyword searches through Google's AdWords site. For example, if you are selling designer T-shirts, you can try a search with those keywords or words close to them. The results will tell you how many people locally and globally have searched on the Internet for those keywords each month. It will also give you a rough idea of market interest in your idea.

1 Go to adwords.google.co.uk.

2 Click Get keyword ideas.

ALERT: If you plan on selling only in the UK, pay particular attention to the local search results you receive, which may differ from the global results.

HOT TIP: This is not an exact way to gauge market interest. However, if you find your search returns no results for your keywords, you may need to rethink your business idea.

3 Enter a word or phrase and select a category if relevant.

4 Enter the encryption code.

5 Click Search and review the results for your keyword.

Find keywords

Based on one or more of the following:

Word or phrase	designer T-shirts 3
Website	www.google.co.uk/page.html
Category	Apparel

☐ Only show ideas closely related to my search terms ⑦

⊞ Advanced Options and Filters | Locations:United Kingdom ✕ | Languages:English ✕ | Devices: Desktops and laptops

Type the characters that appear in the picture below.
Or sign in to get more keyword ideas tailored to your account. ⑦

14.00   mewsbc

| 0041 mewsbc | 4 |

Letters are not case-sensitive

| Search | 5 |

About this data ⑦

| Download ▼ | View as text ▼ | More like these ▼ | | Sorted by Relevance ▼ | Columns ▼ |

⊟ Search Terms (1)

☐	Keyword	Competition	Global Monthly Searches ⑦	Local Monthly Searches ⑦
☐ ☆	designer t-shirts	High	90,500	14,800

Go to page: 1   Show rows 50 ▼ |◄ ◄ 1 - 1 of 1 ► ►|

⊟ Keyword ideas (100)

☐	Keyword	Competition	Global Monthly Searches ⑦	Local Monthly Searches ⑦
☐ ☆	designer t shirts	High	90,500	14,800
☐ ☆	mens designer t shirts	High	4,400	2,400
☐ ☆	designer t shirt	High	90,500	14,800
☐ ☆	designer t shirts for men	High	6,600	3,600
☐ ☆	designer shirt	High	165,000	33,100
☐ ☆	designer shirts	High	165,000	40,500
☐ ☆	designer t shirts men	High	6,600	3,600
☐ ☆	cheap designer t shirts	High	2,400	1,000
☐ ☆	graphic design t shirts	High	8,100	720
☐ ☆	men s designer t shirts	High	260	91
☐ ☆	design t shirts	High	673,000	74,000
☐ ☆	designer shirts mens	High	18,100	9,900
☐ ☆	design own t shirt	High	165,000	33,100
☐ ☆	design t shirts uk	High	3,600	3,600
☐ ☆	designer shirts for men	High	22,200	12,100

★ Starred (0)

Tip 2: Choose an all-in-one domain and site-building package

There are several companies that provide domain name registration, web hosting and website-building tools all in one package. The companies listed below offer easy-to-use website-building tools that you can use through your web browser. You won't need to download or buy any software and you develop a website from a selection of templates which you can change and customise. Check to see whether or not free phone support is offered with the package you choose.

- Moonfruit.com offers a browser-based website-creation tool and has a low-cost website option from £36 per year. There is also a free website option and a free trial period.
- GoDaddy.com has an e-commerce site-building tool called Quick Shopping Cart. You can register a domain name, host your site, get a business email and build your website from £84 annually.
- Easily.co.uk offers domain registration, email, hosting and a website-creator package called EasilyShop. Packages start from £99 annually.
- Actinic.co.uk has an online site-building tool and you can also register and host your domain through the site. Packages start at £228 per year and there is a free 30-day trial.

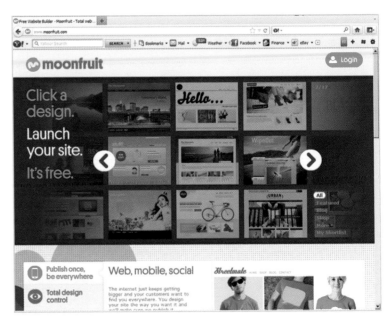

! ALERT: If you choose a free or low-cost option, you usually have to display ads on your webpage.

? DID YOU KNOW? If you have already registered a domain through another registrar, you can transfer it to a new hosting service.

Tip 3: Consider creating a logo

A logo will help brand your business and make it creditable. You can use the logo on your website as well as on any printed marketing material you use such as business cards, packing slips or stationery. You can try to make a logo yourself but some small design businesses will generate a logo design for you for less than £100. Bear the following in mind when coming up with a logo idea for your business.

- Make the logo fit into the business sector you are targeting (technology, fashion, construction, etc.).
- Think about your target market: young people, knitting enthusiasts, gardeners, etc. and make the design and font appealing to them.
- Consider how you will incorporate the colour and design into your website design.
- Look at what other businesses in your sector have done with their logos (but avoid copying them).
- Avoid including free clip art in the logo itself as it will appear amateurish.

Style Ts

✚ Style Ts

Style Ts

HOT TIP: Shop around for a small design firm. Some will offer special deals such as free business cards or business stationery as part of the package.

HOT TIP: A good logo design will reproduce well on a variety of media, including your website, business cards or stationery.

Tip 4: Register for a PayPal account

In order to do business online, you need to have a way to receive money from your customers. Many online shoppers already have a PayPal account and trust this method of payment as it's one of the best known and most widely used. It works when you place a Buy button on your website. When customers click it, it takes them to PayPal and a secure window to provide their payment details. All you need to register is an email address and a credit card.

- Consider selecting the Website Payments Standard option. Your customers can use their credit cards as well as their PayPal account.

- Read through the details of the other options offered by PayPal to see what fits your business.

- Use a business email to register, not your personal email.

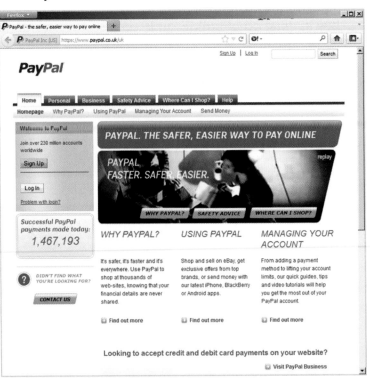

SEE ALSO: Chapter 7 will explore other online payment options and ways to conduct secure transactions on your website.

ALERT: You will pay a fee to use PayPal. The fees vary but are generally a percentage of your sales.

ALERT: There may be other electronic payment systems that came with your website package. You can use those as well as offering a PayPal option to your customers.

Tip 5: Keep in contact with your customers

If you have a list of customers from either your bricks-and-mortar store or from your online store, make sure that you keep them up to date with any changes, additions or special offers you are promoting. You want to create repeat customers and also encourage them to share information about you with their friends and family (your future customers).

- Send a follow-up note a few weeks after a customer buys something to check they are happy or let them know about a related product they may be interested in.
- Let them know about any special offers.
- Send information about new products.
- Update them with changes to your website (e.g. adding an information section or blog).

! ALERT: Don't bombard your customers with emails. Schedule a regular email newsletter, perhaps once or twice a month or when you have something new in stock or run a promotion.

? DID YOU KNOW? If anyone asks not to receive emails from your business you must, by law, honour the request and remove them from your mailing list.

Tip 6: Understand SEO

Search engine optimisation (SEO) is the process of getting your website listed in search engine results for specific keywords. For example, if you have an organic skincare business, you want your website displayed near the top of the search results when a consumer searches for 'organic skincare'. Search engines such as Google, Yahoo! and Bing base their rankings in part on the keywords their computers find on the millions of websites they analyse. In fact, their computers (called crawlers, bots or spiders) trawl through the Internet looking for websites – you don't have to do anything to be found by them. Some key points about SEO include the following.

- Find the best keywords for your business.
- Embed the relevant keywords within your site to get the search engines to find them.
- Have your site linked from other sites (called inbound links).
- Update and change your content often (i.e. a static site with little change in content will rank lower in the results).

HOT TIP: Reach out to other businesses, blogs or websites of friends who may have an interest in linking your website with theirs. Inbound links affect how your site is ranked in the results (the more links, the better).

? DID YOU KNOW?
Adding a blog or an information section to your website and updating it frequently is a good way to add dynamic content to your site.

Tip 7: Protect your business information on a shared computer

Ideally, you will have a computer in your home office exclusively dedicated to your business. However, when you start out you may find yourself sharing this valued resource with others in your household. Be aware that other users can inadvertently move or even delete important files and there are steps you should take to protect your business. You can set up a separate user account for others to use and also add a password to protect your user account so that nobody else will access it.

Here's how to create a new user account.

1 From the Start menu select Control Panel and then User Accounts.

2 Click Manage another account and click Create a new account.

3 Enter a user account name next to Standard user.

4 Click Create Account.

5 Click the Start menu and select Switch user from the menu.

To add a password to your user account, follow these steps.

6 Return to User Accounts and click Create a password for your account.

7 Enter your password, create a hint and click Create password.

? DID YOU KNOW?

If you have a Mac, you can add or change user accounts in System Preferences under Users and Groups. Click the plus (+) symbol to add a new account.

HOT TIP: Create secure passwords with a combination of numbers, letters and symbols and change them frequently.

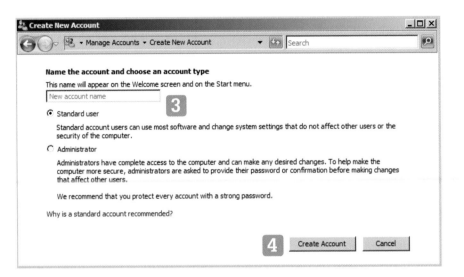

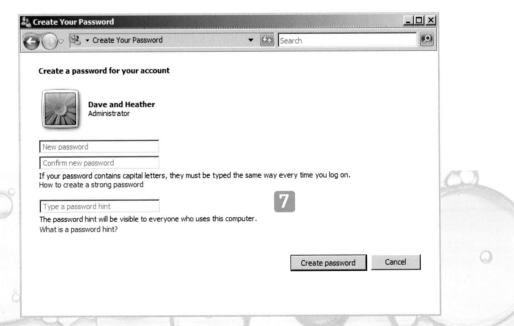

Tip 8: Understand eBay business basics

As an eBay business, you can choose either fixed-price or auction-style listings as you would with an individual account. When you register as a business on the site you need to provide valid contact details as well as details of a bank account that can accept direct debit instructions. If you are registered for VAT, you'll provide your VAT registration number to set up your business account. Other eBay business basics to bear in mind include the following.

- You can't sell your business goods as an individual – you must register for a business account.

- You pay a lower listing fee as a business but you still have to pay a final-value fee if your item sells.

- You are subject to the same feedback rating system as individual sellers and must strive to provide good customer service to earn positive feedback.

- There are several types of shop you can open up as a business, for which you pay a monthly fee.

SEE ALSO: Go to ebay.co.uk/businesscentre/index.html for more information on how to register as a business.

HOT TIP: You don't have to make use of the Shop service but there are advantages to going this route, including discounts on your listing fees. After you spend a few months selling on eBay, consider investing the £14.99 a month for an eBay shop.

Tip 9: Understand Amazon marketplace

Consumers will see only one listing for any given item but are offered a number of sellers to buy from. Customers use Amazon's secure check-out and their experience of shopping will be the same as it would be if they were buying directly from Amazon. Sellers agree to ship the item within 48 hours of a sale. To see how marketplace listings are displayed, do the following.

1 Search for an item that you stock or some other item from the main search box.

2 Click on the link under More Buying Choices.

3 Review the price and delivery costs on offer from each marketplace seller.

All 1-15 of 34 offers

Price + Delivery	Condition	Seller Information	Buying Options
£5.31 + £2.80 delivery 3	New	Seller: **The Book Depository Ltd** Seller Rating: ★★★★★ **98% positive** over the past 12 months. (2,462,341 total ratings) In stock. Dispatched from United Kingdom. International & domestic delivery rates and return policy. Brand New. Shipped from UK Mainland. Delivery is usually 3 - 4 working days from order by Royal Mail, International Delivery ... » Read more	Add to Basket or Sign in to turn on 1-Click ordering.
£5.32 + £2.80 delivery	New	Seller: **ioub** Seller Rating: ★★★★★ **96% positive** over the past 12 months. (656 total ratings) In stock. Dispatched from United Kingdom. Expedited delivery available. International & domestic delivery rates and return policy. Perfect condition. Despatched via First Class Post/Airmail	Add to Basket or Sign in to turn on 1-Click ordering.
£8.15 & this item **Delivered FREE in the UK** with Super Saver Delivery. See details and conditions Eligible for ✓Prime Learn more	New	**amazon**.co.uk In stock. Want guaranteed delivery by 1pm Tuesday, March 27? Order it in the next 22 hours and 4 minutes, and choose **Express Delivery** at checkout. See details Domestic delivery rates and return policy.	Add to Basket or Sign in to turn on 1-Click ordering.
£5.56 + £2.80 delivery	New	Seller: **thebumperbook** Seller Rating: ★★★★★ **98% positive** over the past 12 months. (21,484 total ratings) In stock. Dispatched from United Kingdom. Expedited delivery available. Domestic delivery rates and return policy. In Stock, all UK orders despatched SAME WORKING DAY. Items over 25GBP sent via FedEx. Email support for all customers.	Add to Basket or Sign in to turn on 1-Click ordering.

! ALERT: Pricing is very competitive. Your item and price are listed next to potentially dozens of other providers.

? DID YOU KNOW? Customers are encouraged, but not required, to leave feedback on their transaction with you.

Tip 10: Understand e-commerce regulations

As with other types of commerce, any business you conduct online is subject to a number of different regulations. Most businesses operating online will be subject to E-Commerce Regulations (ECRs) and Distance Selling Regulations (DSRs) and, depending on your business, Provision of Service Regulations (PSRs). These laws are designed to protect consumers who shop online. Below is a basic summary of how the regulations may affect your business – you should take further steps to learn about them. Anyone who sells or advertises goods or services online must comply with the regulations.

- Provide consumers with clear information about your business on your website, including your full contact details, VAT number if you are subject to VAT, clear indication of prices, taxes or postage charges they may incur.

- Outline for customers before they place an order how they can change or cancel an order and when they'll receive an order confirmation.

- Include details of any trade register and the registration number if applicable.

ALERT: Distance trading law allows consumers to cancel and return their order after seven days. There are some exceptions allowed for perishable goods, software that has been opened and flowers, among others.

SEE ALSO: For more information on the laws that apply to your online businesses, go to the Office of Fair Trading website at oft.gov.uk and download more information about the types of regulations outlined above.

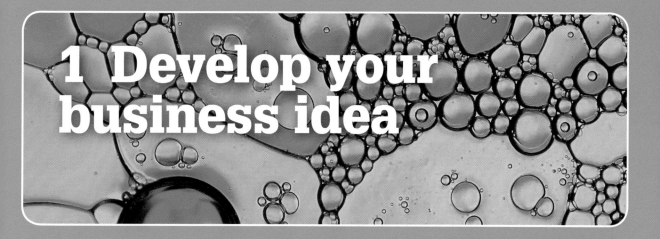

1 Develop your business idea

Introduction

If you are in business, or want to be, having a website is essential to marketing your business and reaching the growing number of people who shop for products or services online. Millions in the UK now do at least some of their shopping online, and that will only increase as confidence in online transactions continues to grow and consumers take advantage of the convenience of shopping online. In addition to the benefit of reaching new customers, the costs associated with starting up an online business are much lower than for a bricks-and-mortar store. If you are still developing a business idea, this chapter will help you refine that idea and develop a working business plan for your new venture.

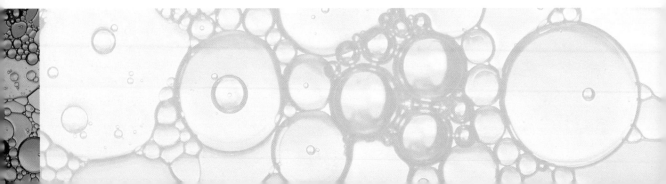

Choose a product or service

Ideally, the business you have in mind is something you are either knowledgeable about or have a keen interest in. It could be something that meets consumers' needs in an original way (though truly novel business ideas are hard to come by) or a service you have been providing while working for an existing company. Even if your idea is not completely new, you should choose something that you will enjoy doing and you think there is a market for. Below are some examples of the types of businesses that you can start up online.

Products

- Handmade cards or jewellery
- Computer games
- Clothing
- Information products (how-to guides, etc.)

Services

- Marketing and graphic design
- Dog walking
- Odd-jobs man
- Speciality construction

ALERT: If you decide you want to sell products, focus on items that are not easily found on the high street.

HOT TIP: Think about the potential postage and storage cost of items you want to sell as you will be posting them yourself. Larger items, such as antiques, are expensive to post and store.

HOT TIP: Don't try to sell a large variety of items as they will be difficult to stock and you won't be able to compete with the large 'mega' stores that already offer them and at a lower cost than you could manage.

Adapt your existing business

If you have an existing business or have experience selling your services or products in the 'real world', you may need to adapt your business slightly to the Web. Having thousands of products online can be costly and time-consuming. You may also find that some products and services will sell better than others or you have a slightly different customer base online.

- Focus on featuring and selling your most popular items.
- Promote those items with the highest profit margin.
- Act as an information source for your customers. For example, consider planning an information section, blog or Frequently Asked Questions (FAQ) page on your website.

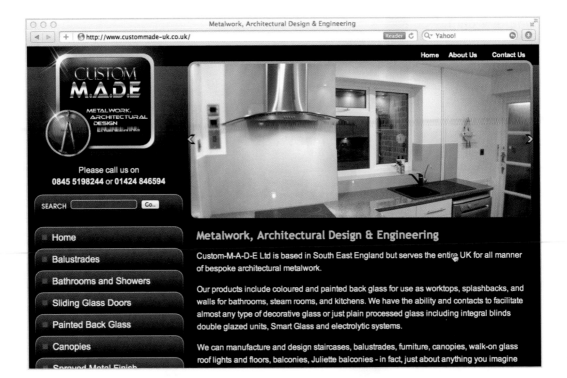

HOT TIP: Keep track of your present customers. If you have a database of existing customers, be sure to get their email details and ask whether or not they would be interested in learning about your website and the special deals you plan to offer there.

Study the market

If there are other businesses already selling the same product or service, look at their websites, study what they offer and see what is selling well. While you do the research, think about things that you can do to differentiate your business from others. In addition, try to find out about your customers, who they are, where they currently shop and how much they usually pay.

- Do a search for other businesses with websites that will be in direct competition with your business.
- Search through active and completed eBay listings.
- Look at amazon.co.uk and research items similar to yours and note how your future competition is pricing and listing items.

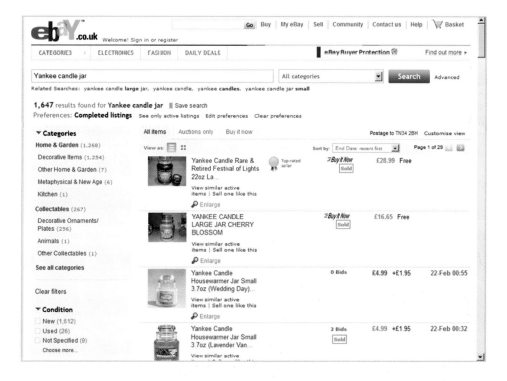

Assess demand for your idea

You can find out how many people are searching the Internet for a specific item by looking at keyword searches through Google's AdWords site. For example, if you are selling designer T-shirts, you can try a search with those keywords or words close to them. The results will tell you how many people locally and globally have searched on the Internet for those keywords each month. It will also give you a rough idea of market interest in your idea.

1 Go to adwords.google.co.uk

2 Click Get keyword ideas.

3 Enter a word or phrase and select a category if relevant.

4 Enter the encryption code.

5 Click Search and review the results for your keyword.

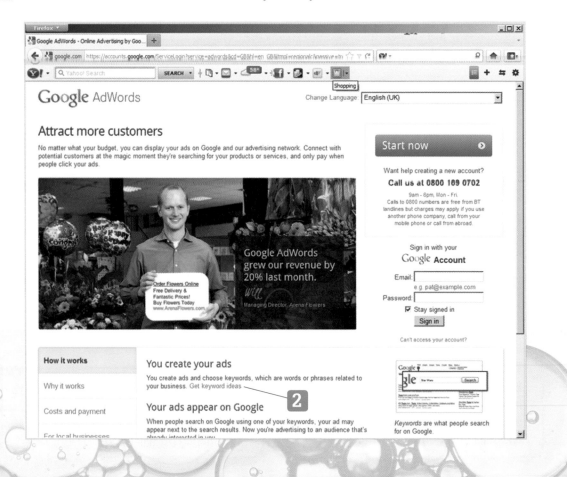

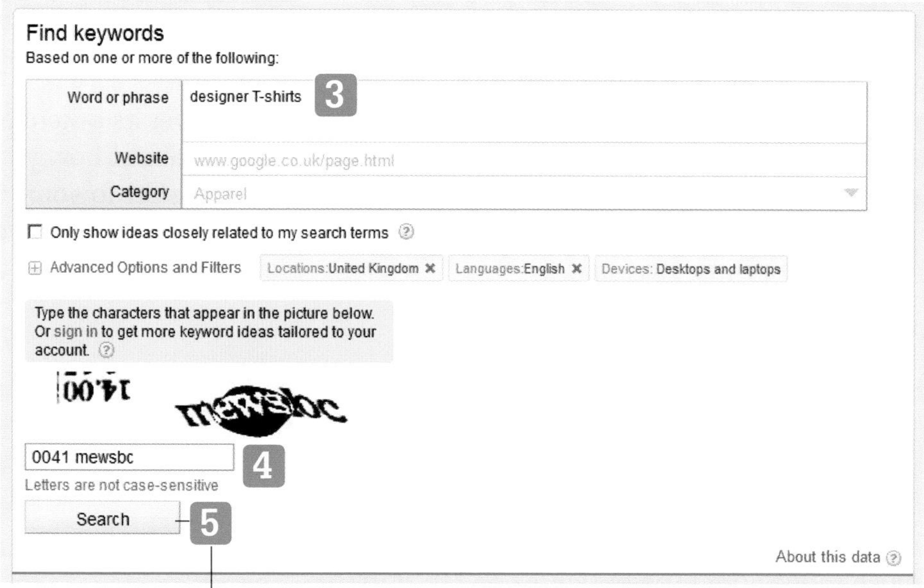

Find keywords

Based on one or more of the following:

Word or phrase	designer T-shirts **3**
Website	www.google.co.uk/page.html
Category	Apparel

☐ Only show ideas closely related to my search terms ⑦

⊞ Advanced Options and Filters   Locations:United Kingdom ✕   Languages:English ✕   Devices: Desktops and laptops

Type the characters that appear in the picture below. Or sign in to get more keyword ideas tailored to your account. ⑦

14.00   mewsbc

| 0041 mewsbc | **4** |

Letters are not case-sensitive

[Search] — **5**

About this data ⑦

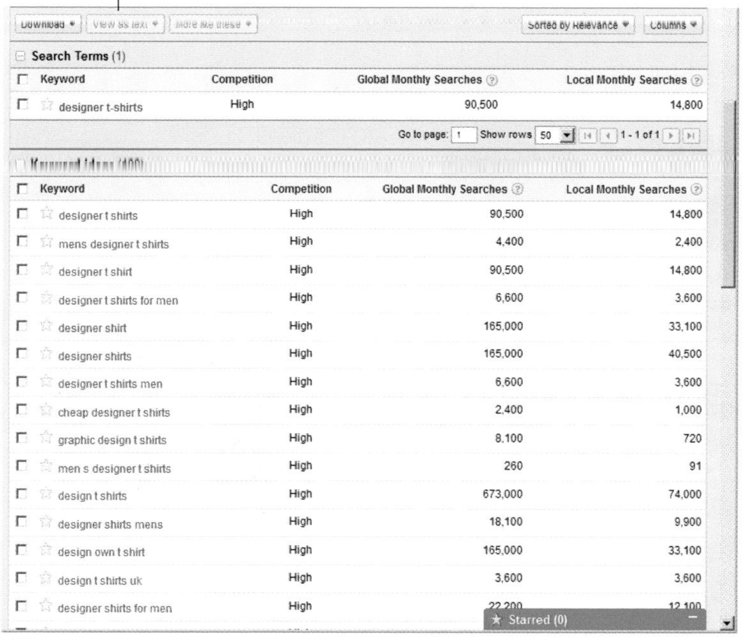

Download ▼   View as text ▼   More like these ▼   Sorted by Relevance ▼   Columns ▼

⊟ Search Terms (1)

☐ Keyword	Competition	Global Monthly Searches ⑦	Local Monthly Searches ⑦
☐ ☆ designer t-shirts	High	90,500	14,800

Go to page: 1   Show rows 50 ▼ |◀ ◀ 1 - 1 of 1 ▶ ▶|

Keyword Ideas (400)

☐ Keyword	Competition	Global Monthly Searches ⑦	Local Monthly Searches ⑦
☐ ☆ designer t shirts	High	90,500	14,800
☐ ☆ mens designer t shirts	High	4,400	2,400
☐ ☆ designer t shirt	High	90,500	14,800
☐ ☆ designer t shirts for men	High	6,600	3,600
☐ ☆ designer shirt	High	165,000	33,100
☐ ☆ designer shirts	High	165,000	40,500
☐ ☆ designer t shirts men	High	6,600	3,600
☐ ☆ cheap designer t shirts	High	2,400	1,000
☐ ☆ graphic design t shirts	High	8,100	720
☐ ☆ men s designer t shirts	High	260	91
☐ ☆ design t shirts	High	673,000	74,000
☐ ☆ designer shirts mens	High	18,100	9,900
☐ ☆ design own t shirt	High	165,000	33,100
☐ ☆ design t shirts uk	High	3,600	3,600
☐ ☆ designer shirts for men	High	22,200	12,100

★ Starred (0)

⚠ **ALERT:** If you plan on selling only in the UK, pay particular attention to the local search results you receive which may differ from the global results.

🔥 **HOT TIP:** This is not an exact way to gauge market interest. However, if you find your search returns no results for your keywords, then you may need to rethink your business idea.

Analyse your business idea

While you may be enthusiastic about your idea, take time to consider its potential strengths and weaknesses. If similar businesses already exist, think about how you will make your business different and what other benefits you can offer to your future customers. If there are any obstacles to setting up your business, consider how you will deal with them before you start up.

Questions to consider before you start:

- Do similar businesses already exist?
- What is unique about my product or service?
- How many customers exist for this idea? Where do they shop currently?
- How often would consumers buy my product or service?
- How much money does the business need to start?

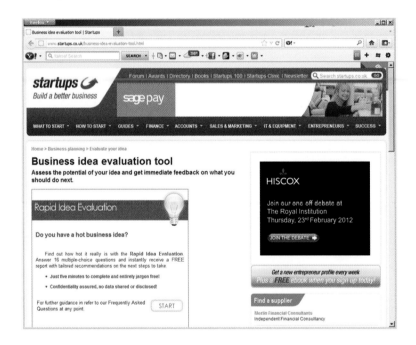

HOT TIP: Start to develop your unique selling point (USP) while in the planning stages. This will be an important part of your business plan if you choose to write one.

SEE ALSO: There is a free business idea evaluation tool at the following website: www.startups.co.uk/business-idea-evaluation-tool.html

Find a supplier

If you plan on offering products to customers, you need to find a reliable wholesaler. Most wholesalers require a minimum order and will sell to businesses only, not members of the public. Check the individual websites of suppliers as each have different requirements for doing business. Be aware that most will sell only in bulk.

- Search the wholesaler index at www.thewholesaler.co.uk and contact a wholesaler for information about their products and prices.
- Attend trade shows and expos.
- Consider shopping at estate sales, charity shops and boot sales if you are interested in selling unique used or antique items.

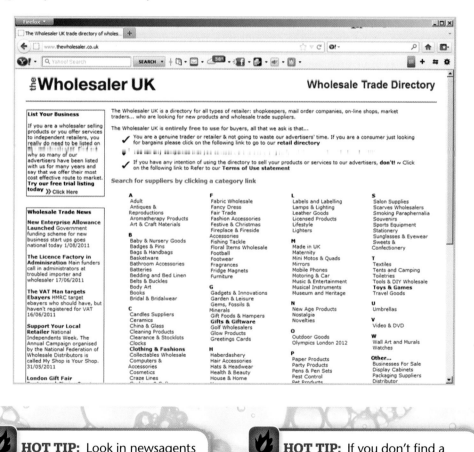

HOT TIP: Look in newsagents for *The Trader* magazine, which lists wholesalers.

HOT TIP: If you don't find a wholesaler you are looking for on the index, do an Internet search with (name of item) + wholesaler.

Assess start-up costs and projected revenues

You need to anticipate what costs you will incur in getting your business off the ground. Think about hardware and the cost of maintaining your computer and Internet connection but also how much you need to spend to get the product you want to your customers – at a profit to you. You can use a simple spreadsheet program to outline your costs and projections.

Take into account the following:

- Office (computer, Internet connection, web hosting and site building).
- Stock to sell.
- Cost of packaging and postage for mailing your products to customers.
- A rough estimate of your projected revenues for the first year of business (retail price minus wholesale price).

	B	C	D
1			
2			
3	**Start Up Costs**		
4			
5	**Description**	**Estimated cost**	
6	Initial order from wholesaler order	£ 1,000.00	
7	Domain registration, hosting and e-commerce builder	£ 200.00	
8	Envelopes and small boxes	£ 150.00	
9	Banking registration, paypal and other	£ 150.00	
10	Money in reserve in case of initial losses	£ 4,000.00	
11			
12		£ 5,500.00	
13			

	A	B	C	D	E	F
1						
2	**Projected Revenue**					
3						
4	**Quarter 1**					
5	Retail cost per unit	# of units	Gross	Costs	Net	
6	£ 20.00	100	£ 2,000.00	£ 800.00	£ 1,200.00	
7						
8	**Quarter 2**					
9	Retail price per unit	# of units	Gross	Costs	Net	
10	£ 20.00	300	£ 6,000.00	£2,700.00	£ 3,300.00	
11						
12	**Quarter 3**					
13	Retail price per unit	# of units	Gross	Costs	Net	
14	£ 20.00	450	£ 9,000.00	£3,600.00	£ 5,400.00	
15						
16	**Quarter 4**					
17	Retail price per unit	# of units	Gross	Costs	Net	
18	£ 20.00	600	£ 12,000.00	£4,800.00	£ 7,200.00	
19						
20					£17,100.00	
21						

ALERT: Even if you make hand-crafted items, you need to account for the supplies you buy to make those products.

ALERT: Keep your projections for the first several months of business very conservative. It will take a while before enough people know about your website and start shopping there.

HOT TIP: Consider whether seasonal sales will affect your business. Is there a period of time when you are less likely to make sales? A period you will be busiest?

Create a business plan

You need a basic road map of where you want to go with your business and a business plan will do just that. Business plans are most commonly created to get a bank loan or find other funding for your business, which you may want to do at some point. However, they can act as a guide for your business when you start out. After you have set up your business, use the plan to check your ongoing progress against your goals and targets and revise your plan as you go. You can write a brief plan on your word-processing program or even on a piece of paper.

Your plan should have the following components:

- Market: who your customers are, what they currently do to buy these products or services, how they pay for these.
- Unique selling point: what your business is going to do differently or better.
- Goals: what you want your business to do and how it will change over time.
- Financials: include your start-up costs and projected revenues for the first year.
- Risks: note any potential problems that you can anticipate. Will you sell more some months than others? Will you be able to secure the same ongoing wholesale prices?

HOT TIP: Use your business plan as a gauge, check your ongoing progress against the plan as you start your business and make changes or adjustments to your plan as needed.

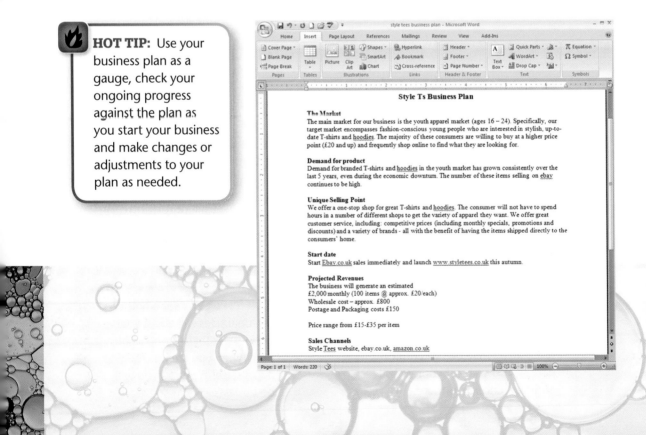

Learn about affiliate/associate programmes

One popular way to generate additional income for your website is through affiliate or associate marketing. An affiliate is another business related to yours that asks to place a small ad or link on your site. You are paid a percentage of the sale when one of your customers clicks that link and goes on to buy a product from your affiliate. For example, if you have a gardening service website you might have an affiliate link for one of your favourite garden supply stores.

Think about the following when considering an affiliate programme on your site:

● Make sure that the affiliate is closely related to your business.

● It should be something that does not compete with items on your website.

● It should be something that you can recommend/believe in.

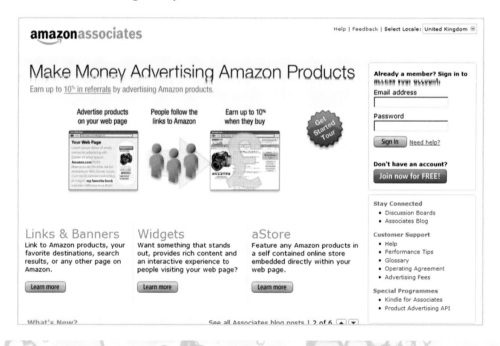

? DID YOU KNOW?
Affiliate programmes are referred to by other names as well. For example, amazon.co.uk calls them associate programmes.

2 Prepare to get your business online

Introduction

It is easier than ever to build a business website without any technical knowledge or special design skills. While you can register a domain, find a web host and buy your own website-building software separately, there are many all-in-one services that provide you with most of the things you need to build a business or e-commerce website. This chapter will walk you through what you need to do to prepare to get your business online, including choosing a provider and preparing the contents of your virtual store.

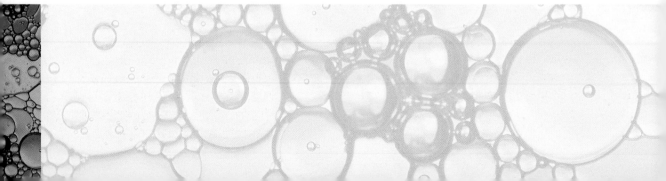

Check your computer's operating system

The website-building packages and programs that are the focus of this book all have some minimum computer operating system requirements. These are general guidelines and the package you choose may have slightly different requirements – once you decide on a provider, check any requirements they have. In general, you need to have an up-to-date operating system for your PC, such as Windows 7, Vista, XP or 2003. For your Mac, you will need to be running Leopard (OS X 10.5) or Snow Leopard (OS X 10.6) or even later.

To check your PC:

1 Go to the Start menu.

2 Select Control Panel.

3 Double-click the System icon.

To check your Mac:

1 Go to the Apple Menu.

2 Select About This Mac.

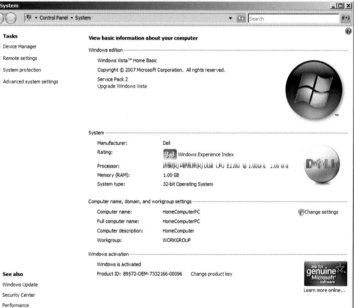

⚠ ALERT: You won't be able to build a website with a dial-up connection. If you don't already have one, look for a broadband provider for your area here: www.broadbrandchoices.co.uk

🔥 HOT TIP: You may want to consider other items for your home office, including a digital camera, scanner and image-editing software to create effective product images for your site.

Update your web browser

In order to use the online website-building tools, you need an up-to-date web browser. Most of the popular web browsers, including Internet Explorer, Firefox, Google Chrome and Safari for Mac, are supported on the web-building sites. Whatever web browser you have, you need to make sure you are running the latest version. The update checks below will search for all your computer updates but will include any updates to your browser.

To update your PC:

1 Click the Start menu and select Control Panel.

2 Double-click Windows Update.

3 Click Check for updates and wait while updates are found.

4 Click Install updates.

To update your Mac:

1 Point your cursor to the Apple menu and select About This Mac.

2 Click Software Update and wait while your Mac looks for updates.

3 Click Continue when prompted and click Install Update.

? DID YOU KNOW?

Developers regularly improve and fix bugs or security problems with your software, including browsers. Checking for and installing updates regularly will improve the functioning of your computer.

! ALERT: You will need to restart your computer after you download the updated browser.

Understand domain names

Your domain name is your website address (greatgiftz.co.uk), the place where customers can find your store on the Internet. You can also use the name as part of your mailing address (e.g. Simon@greatgiftz.co.uk). You may not get the exact name you want so you'll have to experiment with variations of the domain name you have in mind. The top-level domain for the UK is .co.uk but .com domains are also highly sought after.

Follow these tips when developing your domain name:

- Make it easy to remember.
- Check that it is simple (not too many numbers or letters).
- Search on domaincheck.co.uk to see whether or not the name is taken.
- Choose an alternative suffix if .com or .co.uk are taken.

ALERT: Shorter and less complicated names will be more easily picked up by search engines.

HOT TIP: Your name doesn't have to describe your business – you can come up with a fun or interesting name that will stand out in consumers' minds.

Register a domain name

There are thousands of companies and organisations that register domain names (you can find a list on www.nominet.org.uk). Registration usually costs between £5 and £10 per year but some domains (.com) are more expensive than others. You register and pay for a specific name and can keep it as long as you need it – and pay for it.

- Register a domain when you choose a website builder.
- Check whether or not you can register a domain name through your Internet service provider (ISP).
- Register through one of the domain registry sites listed on Nominet.

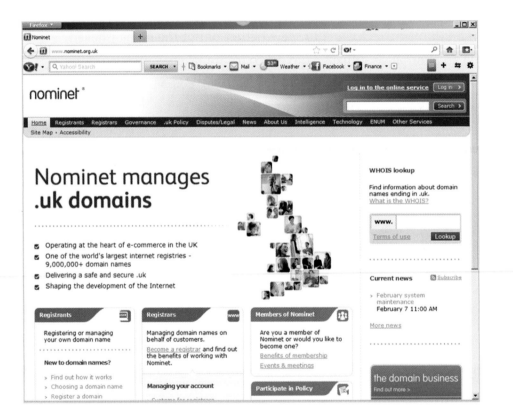

ALERT: When you register a domain ending in co.uk, you have to enter a contact name and address. The information you enter will be publicly available on the WHOIS database for the UK (see the Nominet site for details on this). There are private registration options for other domain extensions, including .com and .org.

SEE ALSO: See the section in this chapter on choosing a website-building package.

Understand web hosting

A web host stores your website on a server (a type of large computer) that is always connected to the Internet. You are effectively renting space on the Internet from a web host. The annual cost of hosting your page depends on the type of website you want. In general, the cost of web hosting will run from £70 to £150 per year.

- Check whether or not your ISP offers a low-cost web-hosting option.
- Consider web hosting through a site-building service.
- Check whether or not you get a discount on hosting when you choose a website-building package.

Choose an all-in-one domain and site-building package

There are several companies that provide domain name registration, web hosting and website-building tools all in one package. The companies listed below offer easy-to-use website-building tools that you can use through your web browser. You won't need to download or buy any software and you develop a website from a selection of templates which you can change and customise. Check to see whether or not free phone support is offered with the package you choose.

- Moonfruit.com offers a browser-based website-creation tool and has a low-cost website option from £36 per year. There is also a free website option and a free trial period.

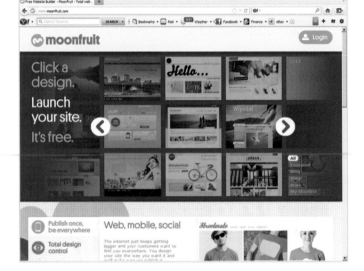

- GoDaddy.com has an e-commerce site-building tool called Quick Shopping Cart. You can register a domain name, host your site, get a business email and build your website from £84 annually.

- Easily.co.uk offers domain registration, email, hosting and a website-creator package called Easilyshop. Packages start from £99 annually.

- Actinic.co.uk has an online site-building tool and you can also register and host your domain through the site. Packages start at £228 per year and there is a free 30-day trial.

ALERT: If you choose a free or low-cost option, you usually have to display ads on your webpage.

? DID YOU KNOW?
If you have already registered a domain through another registrar, you can transfer it to a new hosting service.

HOT TIP: If you regularly sell on ebay.co.uk or amazon.co.uk or plan to, these companies offer additional tools to integrate all your 'shops' into your new website. However, you will pay more for this added feature.

Prepare product descriptions

As consumers can't physically see and touch the products you have to sell, it's important that you describe your product in detail. You may have been provided with basic information from a wholesaler and possibly the European Article Unit (EAN); however, you should expand on those so that your customers know what they are getting. Think about what you want to know about an item when you are shopping online.

- Be concise; consider listing your product's features in a bulleted list.
- Include information about the product weight and dimensions.
- Note if the sizes are smaller or larger than average (if selling clothing or shoes).
- Suggest other ways for the customer to use the item.

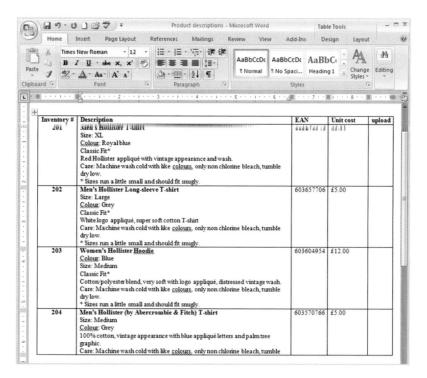

HOT TIP: Use a word-processing program or spreadsheet to write and store descriptions of your items so that you can simply cut and paste them into your website when you build it.

5 901234 123457 >

? DID YOU KNOW?

If you are selling media such as CDs, DVDs or books, there will be an ISBN associated with it which you should take note of. EANs and ISBNs will make it easy for you to create sales listings of your items if you decide to sell on ebay.co.uk or amazon.co.uk

WHAT DOES THIS MEAN?

EAN and ISBN: numbers that uniquely identify consumer products. You see them beneath a barcode on product tags in shops. ISBN is specific to books, CDs and DVDs while EAN covers retail goods in general.

Take photos of your products

If your wholesaler or manufacturer didn't provide you with images for use on your website, you can easily take pictures yourself. There are a few guidelines that you should follow to ensure that your product images are clear and well presented. Use a tripod if you have one or place your digital camera on a steady surface for the best results.

- Take pictures using natural light.
- Use a white or neutral background.
- Fill most of the frame with the product
- Take more than one picture (i.e. different angles or details).

! ALERT: If your item is very small or has many details that you want to highlight for your customers, you need to use the macro mode on your digital camera.

Consider creating a logo

A logo will help brand your business and make it creditable. You can use the logo on your website as well as on any printed marketing material you use such as business cards, packing slips or stationery. You can try to make a logo yourself but some small design businesses will generate a logo design for you for less than £100. Bear the following in mind when coming up with a logo idea for your business.

- Make the logo fit into the business sector you are targeting (technology, fashion, construction, etc.).
- Think about your target market – young people, knitting enthusiasts, gardeners, etc. – and make the design and font appealing to them.
- Consider how you will incorporate the colour and design into your website design.
- Look at what other businesses in your sector have done with their logos (but avoid copying them).
- Avoid including free clip art in the logo itself as it will appear amateurish.

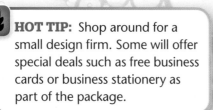

HOT TIP: Shop around for a small design firm. Some will offer special deals such as free business cards or business stationery as part of the package.

HOT TIP: A good logo design will reproduce well on a variety of media, including your website, business cards and stationery.

Register for a PayPal account

In order to do business online, you need to have a way to receive money from your customers. Many online shoppers already have a PayPal account and trust this method of payment as it's one of the best known and most widely used. It works when you place a Buy button on your website. When customers click it, it takes them to PayPal and a secure window to provide their payment details. All you need to register is an email address and a credit card.

- Consider selecting the Website Payments Standard option. Your customers can use their credit cards as well as their PayPal account.
- Read through the details of the other options offered by PayPal to see what fits your business.
- Use a business email to register, not your personal email.

SEE ALSO: Chapter 7 will explore other online payment options and ways to conduct secure transactions on your website.

ALERT: You will pay a fee to use PayPal. The fees vary but are generally a percentage of your sales.

ALERT: There may be other electronic payment systems that came with your website package. You can use those as well as offering a PayPal option to your customers.

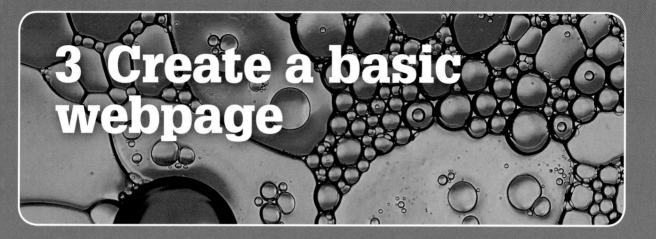

3 Create a basic webpage

Introduction

Many of the online website-building tools make it relatively easy and straightforward to get a site up and running quickly, especially if you already have your product descriptions and images prepared. This chapter focuses on building the basics of a retail or e-commerce site, including adding information about your business, adding products and including images. The examples throughout are from Go Daddy's Quick Shopping Cart. What you see here will be different from your provider's; however, the basic components of an e-commerce site (products, payment and postage options), as well as the strategies for building your site, will be the same.

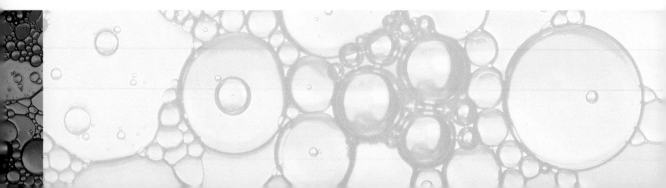

Set up your Quick Shopping Cart account

To get started on building your website, you have to set up your account and specify the domain name you want to use. The steps below take just a few minutes but must be completed before you can start to build your new web store. Once you have logged into your account with your username and password, do the following:

1 Click on My Account.

2 Scroll to My Products and click Quick Shopping Cart.

3 Click Open next to your account.

4 Click Accept after reading the licence agreement.

5 Select your domain name and enter your details.

6 Enter your PayPal email address and click OK.

ALERT: If you do not have a PayPal account, you will need to set one up before you launch your site. See Chapter 2 for information on this.

Start Quick Shopping Cart

Go Daddy has several tabs called Quick Access buttons that remain at the top of Quick Shopping Cart while you are building your site. The buttons outline the steps you need to take to build your site, including basic store information, template design, postage options, and product descriptions and costs. Once you publish your site, these tabs will disappear. You can still edit any part of your website by using the menu items at the top of the page (Set Up, Manage, Promote, etc.).

To start the Shopping Cart builder:

1 Click on the My Account tab.

2 Click on Quick Shopping Cart.

3 Click Launch next to your Quick Shopping Cart account.

4 Point your cursor at the menu items to view the drop-down menu.

5 If you navigate away from where you want to be, click Home to return to the main menu.

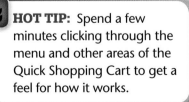

HOT TIP: Spend a few minutes clicking through the menu and other areas of the Quick Shopping Cart to get a feel for how it works.

Edit your store information and add a logo

You can enter more details about your shop by using the Quick Access buttons. You may have entered some of this information when you set up your account but check again that you have included all the details you want to. You can also upload a logo if you have one under this section.

1 Click Edit on the Storefront Information button.

2 Enter your contact information and other details.

3 Scroll down to the Logo Upload section.

4 Click Upload and locate the image on your computer.

5 Select Scale to fit and click OK.

6 Click OK to save the changes.

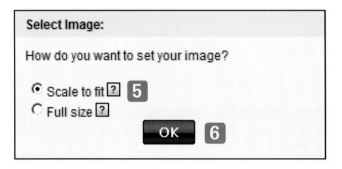

HOT TIP: Consider adding a mailing address and telephone number to your site. Customers feel more confident shopping online if they have an alternative way to contact a business.

HOT TIP: You can click the Preview tab in the upper right corner at any time to see the changes to your website.

Customise your website template

You will have a default template attached to your store when you first log into Quick Shopping Cart. However, you don't have to keep this template – you can browse for a style that better suits your business idea as well as customise your colour scheme.

1 Click Edit on the Templates button.

2 Click the arrow to browse through template options

or

3 choose a category type to filter your option (Minimalist, Dark, Cute, etc.).

4 Select a colour option for that template.

5 Click Apply to My Store.

6 Click on Preview to see the changes to your page.

ALERT: Clicking on Publish will upload your site to the Internet where it can be seen by others. Wait until your store is complete before publishing.

Understand VAT obligations

You may see a Quick Start button that includes adding taxes to your product listings. If you are responsible for VAT it has to be included in the listing price of the item, not calculated after a sale (as is the case for US-based businesses). Most UK businesses that reach a certain sales threshold (currently around £73,000) are required to include VAT on their items. There are several exceptions to this and it is unlikely that many small businesses will reach the upper threshold in the first several years of business. However, you must take steps to understand your potential tax obligations. Do the following:

1 Go to www.hmrc.gov.uk/vat/index.htm and review VAT policies that apply to your business.

2 Call a local VAT office for free advice on whether you should register.

3 Enlist the help of a business tax accountant.

? DID YOU KNOW? If you are liable for VAT, all submissions have to be filed online with the HMRC.

▶ SEE ALSO: You may have other tax obligations depending on what type of business you have. See Chapter 10 for more information on this.

Add postage options to your site

Once you make a sale, you need to get your items to your customers. Most consumers are keen to receive their items quickly and with the least possible expense. Keep in mind that you may be competing for sales with some of the larger online retail sites. Even if your products are not in competition with some of the larger sites, shoppers are used to receiving their online orders in a few days for a reasonable fee. There are two easy options to choose from, including a flat rate for all your items or charging a percentage rate based on the product dimensions and weight.

1 Click Edit on the Shipping Quick Access button.

2 Click the Set Up button next to one of the Easy options.

3 Name the type of postage rate (flat or percentage).

4 Enter a shipping fee.

5 Add a regional or postal code surcharge if you wish.

6 Click OK to save changes.

Shipping Method	Flat Rate	Real-Time	International	Weight-Based	Requires Dimensions	Actions
Flat Rate (%) Easy	●		●			Set Up
Flat Rate (£) Easy	●		●			on Edit
Custom Shipping Moderate	●		●	●		Set Up

QUICK SHOPPING CART

Dashboard | Site | Store | Blog | Album | Templates

Home | Set Up | Manage | Promote | Report | Favorites | Help

○ **Operations: Shipping Options: Flat Rate (£)**

Set your cart to charge customers a flat rate shipping fee to their order total

Configure Flat Rate (£) Shipping

* Required

Name: *
Flat Rate

Shipping Fee:
£   2.95 added to order total

Regional Surcharges:

Country	Region	Amount
	Add	

Postal Code Surcharges:

Country	Postal Code	Amount
	Add	

OK   Cancel

Enable your PayPal account

The quickest way to start receiving money through your business is via your PayPal account. There is a simple button you need to click to enable payments through your site. If you don't yet have an account, revisit the information on PayPal in Chapter 2.

1 Click Edit on the Payment button.

2 Click Enable on the PayPal button.

3 Enter your PayPal email address.

4 Select a PayPal icon to display in your store.

5 Click OK.

PayPal

PayPal Express Checkout · PayPal can be used as a way to accept both credit cards and PayPal with our hosted option. Also, if you already accept credit cards on your site, accept PayPal as well to boost sales.

With PayPal as an additional payment method, your customers do not need to enter their credit card information. They simply log into their PayPal account and confirm the payment. With PayPal, your customers can choose to pay with credit card, debit card, bank account or their PayPal balance.

Enable **2**

⊞ PayPal Website Payment Standard

COD

⊞ COD   Enable

Print and Call

✓ ⊞ Print and Call   Edit Disable

Simple Setup

Please enter the email address where you want to receive payments: **3**

Let your customers know that you accept PayPal Select an image to add to your footer:

PayPal

4 PayPal

MasterCard VISA AMEX DISCOVER BANK

Optional Setup Enhancement

To add refund and adjustment capability to your PayPal account, you also need to grant us api permissions. To do so, enter the username below in the API Access subsection of PayPal.

Third Party Permissions Username: qsc-ppec_api1.starfieldtech.com

For more assistance, see our Help Document.

Don't have a PayPal Business Account? Set up PayPal now or wait until you receive your first PayPal payment.

5 OK Cancel

HOT TIP: PayPal is the simplest payment option to begin with but you can change to a merchant credit card account later (and after you have an established merchant account).

SEE ALSO: Merchant accounts and other online payment options are explored in Chapter 7.

Add product descriptions

After you create the basic structure of your website with the template and other options, it's time to stock the shelves of your virtual store. You can add and edit products through the Quick Access buttons and also through the menu at the top of the Quick Shopping Cart. Ideally, you will already have descriptions of the products you intend to sell. If not, see Chapter 2 again for information on writing these.

1 Click Edit on the Products Quick Access button.

2 Enter the SKU, the title and add a short description.

3 Enter the full description.

⊟ **Product**

* Required

Product Type: ◉ **Standalone:** Product with one SKU and no variations. ◷

Part Number (SKU): * `603538184` ◷

Inventoried: ◉ No ○ Yes ◷

Charge for Shipping: ○ Yes ◉ No ◷

International Shipping: You have not enabled International Shipping.

○ **Configurable Variations:** Product with a unique SKU for each option. ◷

○ **Bundle:** Combination of standalone products into a bundle with one price. ◷

○ **Downloadable:** Digitally downloadable product. ◷

Title: * `Women's Abercrombie & Fitch T-shirt`

Short Description: *
◷ (300 characters, including HTML tags which are not visible in this editor)

Switch to Standard editor

Women's A&F Dark Pink long-sleeved T-shirt

Path: p

Full Description: *

Switch to Standard editor

Long sleeve, Classic fit*

Size: Medium

100% cotton V-neck, very soft with velvet interior neck tapping and vintage Abercrombie wash.

ALERT: There are default buttons selected that you can leave for now, including Inventoried and Charge for Shipping.

HOT TIP: The short description will display on the category page and the longer description will be on the page for the product itself.

4 Add a manufacturer if relevant and include the UPC, EAN or ISBN if you have it.

5 Enter your List Price (what you will charge customers) and Your Cost.

6 Select No for Taxable if you aren't adding VAT to your products.

7 Click OK.

Manufacturer	Abercrombie & Fitch ▼ **Add Manufacturer**
Manufacturer's Product Number	
Taxable:	○ Yes ● No **6**
Featured:	○ Yes ● No
Hide:	○ Yes ● No
Add to Google Product Search:	○ Yes ● No
Condition:	● New ○ Used ○ Refurbished
UPC:	
EAN:	**4**
ISBN:	

⊟ **Prices:**

Your Cost: £ 8.00
List Price: * £ 22.00 **5**

Add New Sales Price

Want to offer discount pricing for bulk quantities?

⊞ **Category:**

⊞ **Images:**

⊞ **Search Engine Optimization (SEO):**

⊞ **Attributes:**

⊞ **Options:**

⊞ **Up-Sells and Cross-Sells:**

7 **OK**

WHAT DOES THIS MEAN?

SKU: stockkeeping unit, which you can assign to your inventory to track it.

UPC: similar to EAN and ISBN, a way to keep track of each item of inventory.

Upload product images

You should have a collection of digital product images ready to upload. If you don't yet have these on your computer, review the information on taking photographs of your products in Chapter 2.

1 Go to the Manage menu and select Media Gallery from the drop-down menu.

2 Click Upload Images to find the product images on your computer.

3 Shift-click to select multiple images, then click Open or press Enter.

4 Wait while the images upload.

5 Click OK when the upload is complete.

HOT TIP: You can upload a variety of image file formats, including JPEG, TIFF or GIF (extension on your image file will be shown as .jpeg, .tiff or .gif).

Assign images to your products

Depending on the type of account, you can add several photos for each product. If you have the Economy website account, you will have only one photograph for each product, shown in various views (thumbnail, standard and zoom) depending on where they are displayed on the site. Your customers will see the largest image once they click on the actual product page.

1 Go to the Manage menu and select Products from the drop-down menu.

2 Click on the Assign Image icon next to a product.

	Title ▲	Part # (SKU)	Type	List Price	Cur. Sale Price	Inventory	Manufacturer	Featured	Hidden	Actions
☐	Men's Abercrombie &Fitch Muscle T-shirt	604154166	Standard	£22.00	N/A	N/A	No Manufacturer	No	No	
☐	Men's Hollister Long-sleeve T-shirt	603657706	Standard	£20.00	N/A	N/A	No Manufacturer	No	No	
☐	Men's Hollister T-shirt	603276946	Standard	£20.00	N/A	N/A	No Manufacturer	No	No	
☐	Men's Hollister T-shirt	603570766	Standard	£20.00	N/A	N/A	No Manufacturer	No	No	
☐	Women's Abercrombie & Fitch T-shirt	603538184	Standard	£22.00	N/A	N/A	No Manufacturer	No	No	
☐	Women's Hollister Hoodie	603604954	Standard	£32.00	N/A	N/A	No Manufacturer	No	No	

2

HOT TIP: Check that you have a high-resolution image for the close-up (zoom) function to work best.

3 Click and drag the image to the image boxes (thumbnail, standard and zoom).

4 Click OK.

Media Gallery - Women's Abercrombie & Fitch T-shirt

What is the difference between one-image and multi-image?

| One-Image | NEW Multi-Image | Add Images |

| Thumbnail ▶ | Standard | **3** | Zoom | | Use default image |

Click & drag image here

Img206.JPG | Img206.JPG

Search [   ] Search View All   Click and drag image to top.

| IMG_1839.J | IMG_1838.J | IMG_1836.J | IMG_1834.J | IMG_1833.J | IMG_1832.J | IMG_1831.J | IMG_1830.J | IMG_1829.J |

| IMG_1826.J | IMG_1825.J | IMG_1823.J | IMG_1822.J | IMG_1820.J | IMG_1819.J | IMG_1818.J | IMG_1817.J | Img206.JPG |

| Img203.JPG | HolMlrgGry | AFlongslvM | Style Ts | IMG_1827.J | 203.jpg | Img205.JPG | Img204.JPG | Img202.jpg |

Previous 1 2 Next

4 OK Cancel

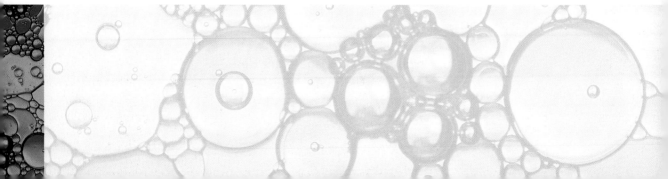

4 Add email and edit your webpage

Introduction

With the basics of your site in place, you can now expand your business by adding a professional email address and editing your welcome message to share with customers what is unique about your store. In the rest of the chapter, you'll learn more about editing and customising your site, including changing the way your products and categories are displayed as well as exploring some of the general editing functions with Go Daddy's Quick Shopping Cart. Finally, you will publish your site when you think it's ready.

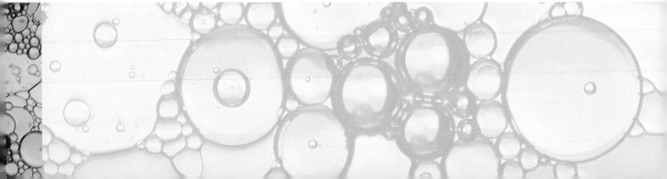

Set up your website email

Now that you have a business website, you need a business email address to go with it so you can communicate with your customers and market your business. Most website packages provide you with an email address that goes with your domain name. In Go Daddy you get up to five email addresses (or more) depending on the package you have chosen.

1. Log into your account and scroll down to Products.

2. Click the plus symbol next to Email (this will then change to a minus sign).

3. Click Set Up next to one of the email accounts.

ALERT: You will have to wait a short time, about 5–10 minutes, before the email account is set up and you can assign a name to it.

4 Select your domain from the drop-down menu (if you have more than one).

5 Click the green Set Up button.

6 Close the window and wait while your email is set up.

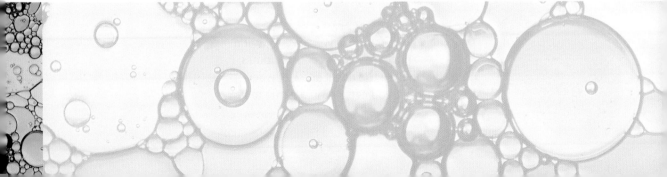

Assign a name to your email

Consider using a first name as a prefix for your business email address as customers generally prefer to feel they are communicating with a person rather than a 'business'. If you have more than one email address, consider adding prefixes that relate to different areas of your business, e.g. information, customer service or account.

1 Log into your account and scroll to Products.

2 Click the plus symbol next to Email.

3 Click Launch next to the email account you set up.

4 Click Add and type in the email name you want.

5 Enter your password twice.

6 Click OK.

Create Mailbox ☒

| Settings | Related Products | Advanced | Auto Reply |

*Required

ⓘ Using Outlook? Start quick setup now.

Email Address:*

contact @ styletees.co.uk ▾

Set Password:* **5** Confirm Password:*

Space for this mailbox:* (1000 MB Available)

1000 MB

☐ Make this mailbox a catchall. What is this?

6 OK Cancel

⚠️ **ALERT:** It takes a few more minutes for the new address to register. Wait a few minutes before launching your new email.

Launch your email

The Go Daddy email account that is associated with your business website is based in your web browser, much like the site-building tools. Go Daddy email is called Workspace. You can access it from your browser when you log into your account and scroll down to your email.

1 Log into your account and scroll to Products.

2 Click the plus symbol next to Email.

3 Click Launch next to your new email account.

4 Click on the envelope icon to launch Webmail.

ALERT: The email account will show as active when it is ready to launch.

5 Read your first welcome message in your inbox.

HOT TIP: The mail program is set up like many other email programs with an inbox, address book and other common features. Take a few minutes to look around your email account and familiarise yourself with it.

SEE ALSO: Chapter 6 will show you how to create email marketing messages to promote your business and let your customers know about special offers.

Edit your welcome message

At the top of your home page there is a default welcome message, which is one of the first things a customer sees when they visit the site. You probably want to change the default message and use this important feature of your website to pitch your business to your customers. Use it to tell customers something about your store or products, the secure payment option(s) available, and what is unique about what you offer.

1 Click Account.

2 Click Launch next to your website in the Quick Shopping Cart.

3 Click the Set Up menu and select Store Home Page.

4 Type over any of the text you don't want and add your own message.

5 Click OK.

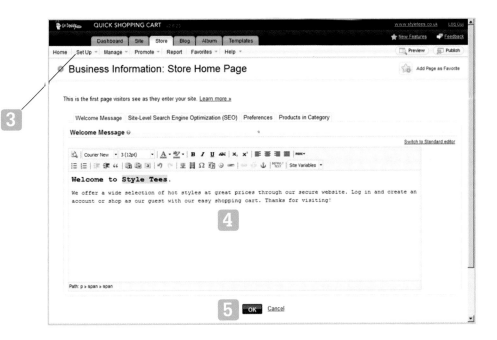

HOT TIP: If you change the font, check it is one that is similar to the style of the rest of the website. Having many different fonts on the page will make it look amateurish.

ALERT: You can't change the highlighted text (store name) in the text box of the welcome message.

Add categories to your site

If you have more than a few items on offer, you will want to set up categories on your website. Without categories to organise your products, the product listings will display in one long list on your home page. When you create categories, there are links on the sidebar of your site. Customers with an interest in a particular product category can click the link and be taken to the category that interests them the most.

Go to your Quick Shopping Cart page:

1 Click Manage from the menu and select Add Category.

2 Assign a name to the category.

3 Write a short description if you wish.

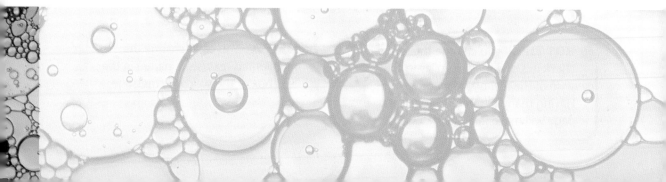

4 Click Choose beneath Standard to assign an image to the category.

5 Select an image from your Image Gallery and click OK.

6 Click OK at the bottom of the Categories page when you've finished.

Standard:

Choose **4**

(Default Image)

Scale To Fit ☉   Full Size ☉

Image Alternate Text:
(250 characters)

Search Engine Optimization (SEO)

Meta Tag Title: Men's T-shirts

Meta Tag Description:
(300 characters)

Meta Tag Keywords:
(1000 characters)

Products in Category ☉

Men's Abercrombie &Fitch Muscle T-shirt (604154166)   Add To List

You currently have no products associated with this category.

DELETE ☒
MOVE UP ⬆
MOVE DOWN ⬇

5 OK

ALERT: You need to add an image to the category or the category will display on the front page as a grey folder icon. Choose one of your most popular (or potentially most popular) products and use that image to represent the product category.

Add products to your categories

Once you have established categories, putting products into those categories is relatively straightforward. From within Quick Shopping Cart, do the following:

1 Click Manage from the menu and select Categories.

2 Click on a category folder.

3 Click Edit Category.

4 Scroll to Products in Category.

5 Select a product from the drop-down list and click Add To List.

6 Add all the selected products to the category and click OK when you've finished.

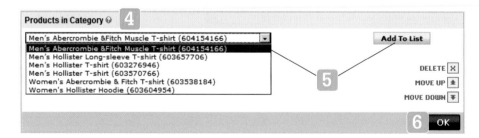

Categories & Products	Type	Quantity	Last Updated
Men's T-shirts	Category	N/A	Sat, Feb 18, 2012 12:01:36
Women's Hoodies	Category	N/A	Sat, Feb 18, 2012 12:09:12
Women's T-Shirts	Category	N/A	Sat, Feb 18, 2012 12:08:18
Men's Abercrombie &Fitch Muscle T-shirt	Standard Product	N/A	Fri, Feb 17, 2012 11:16:28
Men's Hollister Long-sleeve T-shirt	Standard Product	N/A	Fri, Feb 17, 2012 11:13:02
Men's Hollister T-shirt	Standard Product	N/A	Fri, Feb 17, 2012 11:14:31
Men's Hollister T-shirt	Standard Product	N/A	Fri, Feb 17, 2012 11:13:41
Women's Abercrombie & Fitch T-shirt	Standard Product	N/A	Fri, Feb 17, 2012 11:15:33
Women's Hollister Hoodie	Standard Product	N/A	Tue, Jan 31, 2012 20:27:28

Tasks ⌃

- Add Category
- Edit Category —— **3**
- Copy Category
- Move Category
- Delete Category
- Add Product
- Import Products
- Export Products
- Import Images
- Export Images
- Import Option Associations
- Export Option Associations
- File Type Settings

Products in Category ⊙ **4**

Men's Abercrombie &Fitch Muscle T-shirt (604154166) ▼

Men's Abercrombie &Fitch Muscle T-shirt (604154166)
Men's Hollister Long-sleeve T-shirt (603657706)
Men's Hollister T-shirt (603276946)
Men's Hollister T-shirt (603570766)
Women's Abercrombie & Fitch T-shirt (603538184)
Women's Hollister Hoodie (603604954)

Add To List

5

DELETE ✕
MOVE UP ▲
MOVE DOWN ▼

6 OK

HOT TIP: You can include a single product in more than one category folder if it makes sense.

Change category page styles

If you have a number of categories, you can organise them in different ways on your page. You may want to have a border around the category images or perhaps you want them displayed in a wider column. You can customise how they display by following these steps:

1 Click the Set Up menu and select Category Page Style.

2 Scroll through the layout options and click on one to preview it in your page.

3 Click on a style you like.

4 Click OK.

HOT TIP: If there is a lot of white background to your category images, consider selecting the layout with borders around each image to visually define the categories better.

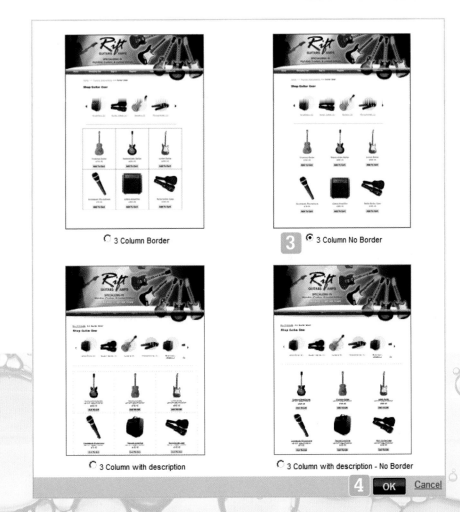

○ 3 Column Border

3 ◉ 3 Column No Border

○ 3 Column with description

○ 3 Column with description - No Border

4 OK Cancel

Change product page styles

The product page displays when a customer clicks on a product for a more detailed view. You can customise the way this displays on your website in much the same way as you changed the category page styles.

1 Click the Set Up menu and select Product Page Styles.

2 Scroll through the options and click on one to preview it on your site.

3 Click on a style you want.

4 Click OK.

HOT TIP: If you have a bold or detailed logo design on one side of the title of your page, consider choosing a product page style that displays the product on the opposite side of the page so that the two images don't compete with one another.

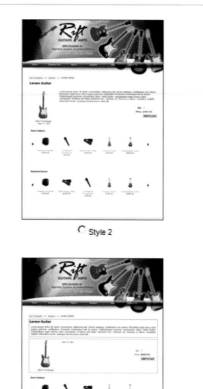

○ Style 2

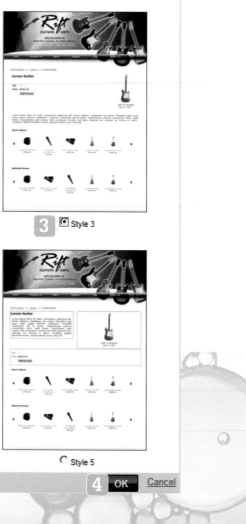

3 ◉ Style 3

○ Style 4

○ Style 5

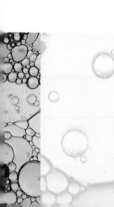

4 OK   Cancel

Edit and add products

If you haven't published your website yet, you can still add and edit products through the Quick Access buttons. If you have published, you can work through the menu to manage your website. From within your Quick Shopping Cart page:

1 Click Manage and select Products.

2 Click Edit next to a product you want to change.

3 Make the required changes to your product listing.

4 Scroll to the bottom of the product page and click OK.

? DID YOU KNOW?

You can permanently delete a product by clicking on the red delete button.

Publish your website

When to publish your website is up to you. With the basic features such as products, payment and postage in place, you could start up at any time. However, you can wait and add more products and features to your site before you publish. It will take a day or two for your website to be available on the Internet so take that into account when planning your launch.

1 Log into your account.

2 Click Launch in your Quick Shopping Cart.

3 Click Publish on the Store Complete button.

4 Click Preview Store to check for any mistakes.

5 Click Start Publish and wait while your site uploads.

6 Click the address of your store once you see Publishing Complete.

Store Complete

Publish

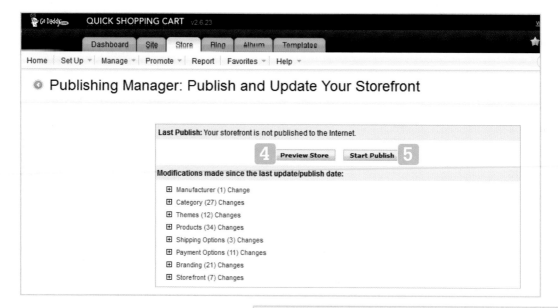

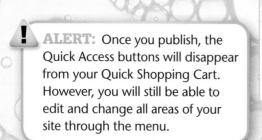

ALERT: Once you publish, the Quick Access buttons will disappear from your Quick Shopping Cart. However, you will still be able to edit and change all areas of your site through the menu.

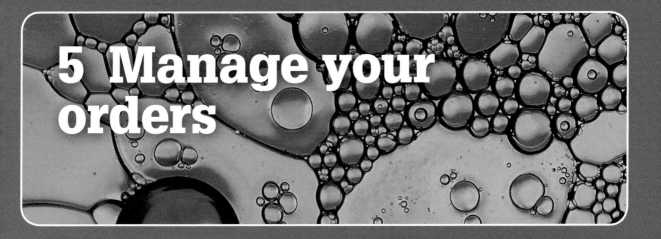

5 Manage your orders

Introduction

The most exciting part of publishing your page is getting your first order. This chapter will show you how to process orders in Quick Shipping Cart and offer tips on how to provide the very best customer service and encourage return customers. There are several administrative steps that you must take in order to keep track of your order, payments as well as posting products to your customers. Finally, we take a look at managing your inventory so that you are always able to offer your customers what they want.

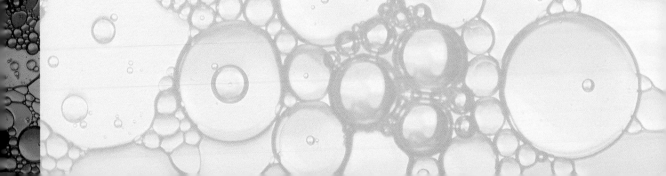

Monitor your orders

After you publish your store, the top of your Quick Shopping will display a Store Summary, which updates you about new orders, inventory alerts or other issues that need your attention. Once you are logged into your Quick Shopping Cart, take these steps:

1 Click New under Order Summary.

2 Click the Edit icon.

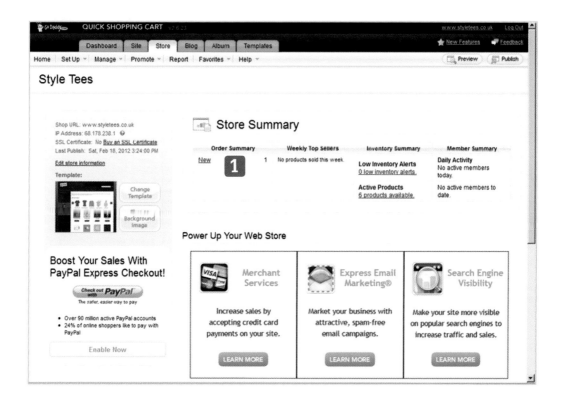

3 View the Order details.

4 Make note of the Payment Type.

5 Make note of the Payment Status.

6 Click OK.

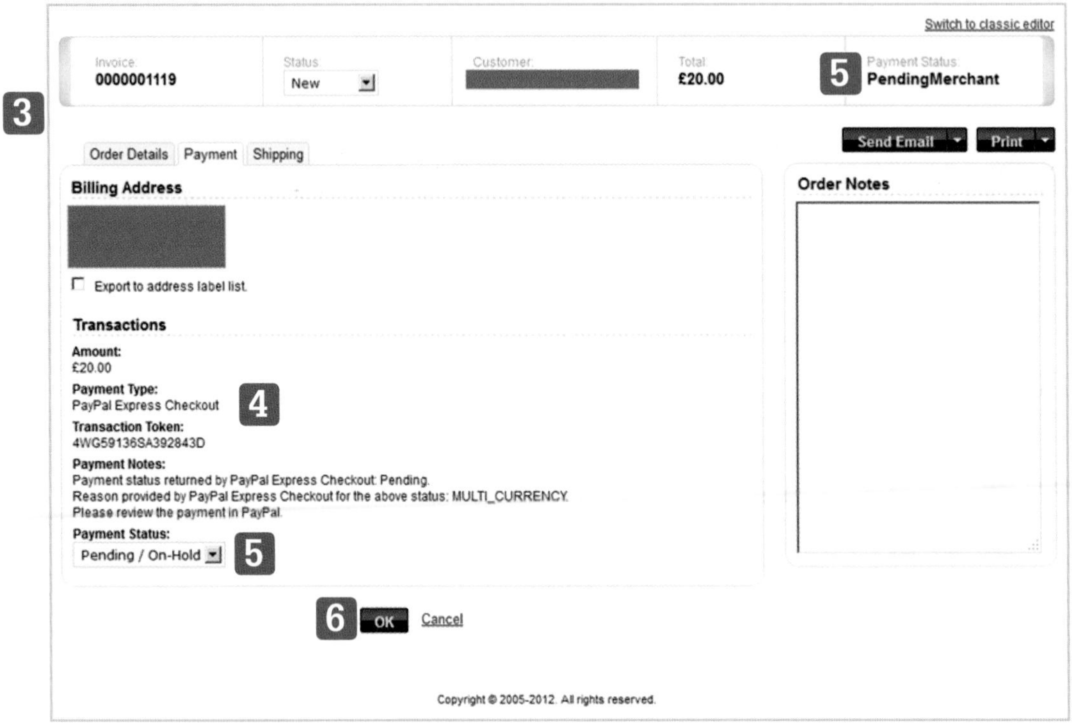

Switch to classic editor

| Invoice 0000001119 | Status New | Customer | Total £20.00 | **5** Payment Status: **PendingMerchant** |

3

Order Details | Payment | Shipping

Send Email ▼   Print ▼

Billing Address

☐ Export to address label list.

Order Notes

Transactions

Amount:
£20.00

Payment Type:
PayPal Express Checkout   **4**

Transaction Token:
4WG59136SA392843D

Payment Notes:
Payment status returned by PayPal Express Checkout: Pending.
Reason provided by PayPal Express Checkout for the above status: MULTI_CURRENCY.
Please review the payment in PayPal.

Payment Status:
Pending / On-Hold ▼   **5**

6 OK   Cancel

? DID YOU KNOW?

The order is automatically assigned an invoice number once an item is purchased – you don't have to generate invoices yourself.

Process a PayPal payment

If your customer bought a product through PayPal, you need to process the order through your PayPal account for it to be complete. You should receive a notification through the email account registered with your PayPal account. You can also just log into paypal.co.uk and check the payment status once you know an order has been placed.

1 Go to the PayPal main page and enter your email address and password.

2 Click Go to My Account.

3 Click Accept. You have to claim the payment from the customer in order to complete the process.

4 Select Accept this payment.

5 Click Submit.

! ALERT: You must accept the payment in order for the funds to be transferred into your account.

? DID YOU KNOW?
PayPal payments usually complete within a few minutes but if you do business internationally, the payment process can take longer.

Buy and print a shipping label

Once you accept the PayPal payment, you can also opt to buy postage through the PayPal site. You can choose a number of postage options through PayPal, including Royal Mail and other providers. If you opt to buy postage online, you need a printer to print out the label and accompanying shipping code.

1 Log into your PayPal account.

2 Click My Account and click Payments received.

3 Click Print shipping label next to the accepted payment.

4 Choose a shipping carrier and click Continue.

5 Enter the addresses and other shipment information and click Continue.

6 Check the address label and purchase your shipping label.

2

	Date		Type	Name/Email	Payment status	Details	Order status/Actions	Net amount
	Feb 19, 2012		Payment From		Unclaimed	Details	Accept ▾	£20.00 GBP
	Feb 19, 2012		Payment From		Completed	Details	Print shipping label ▾ **3**	£19.22 GBP

All activity | All activity (with balance) | Payments received | More filters ▾   In All Currencies ▾

Payments received - Jan 28, 2012 to Feb 27, 2012   Print

Move to Recent Activity   What's this   Payment status glossary

Move to Recent Activity   What's this

HOT TIP: Compare rates and other features of shipping services to choose the best one for your business. Many services such as Royal Mail, Parcelforce and DHL offer online tracking of orders – something customers like.

ALERT: Keep a note of any tracking code if you paid for one so that you can share the tracking information with your customer.

Log payments in your store

Once you have accepted your PayPal payment, log that information into your Quick Shopping Cart account.

1 Click New in your Store Summary or click Manage and select Orders.

2 Click Edit on the order you want to work with.

3 Click on the Payment tab

4 Select Completed under Payment Status.

5 Click OK.

Order Details	Payment	Shipping

Billing Address

3

☐ Export to address label list.

Transactions

Amount:
£20.00

Payment Type:
PayPal Express Checkout

Transaction Token:
4N253359BS5217802

Payment Notes:
Payment status returned by PayPal Express Checkout: Pending.
Reason provided by PayPal Express Checkout for the above status: MULTI_CURRENCY.
Please review the payment in PayPal.

Payment Status:
Pending / On-Hold ▾   **4**
Pending / On-Hold
Completed

5 OK   Cancel

! ALERT: Once you select the Payment Status as Completed, it can't be changed.

Assign a package to an order

This is an administrative step that helps you keep track of your customers' orders. This becomes especially useful when you have more than one item in a package. Complete this process once the payment is accepted into your PayPal account and logged in your store.

1 Click the Manage menu and select Open Orders.

2 Click the Edit icon.

3 Click the Shipping tab.

4 Click Add Package.

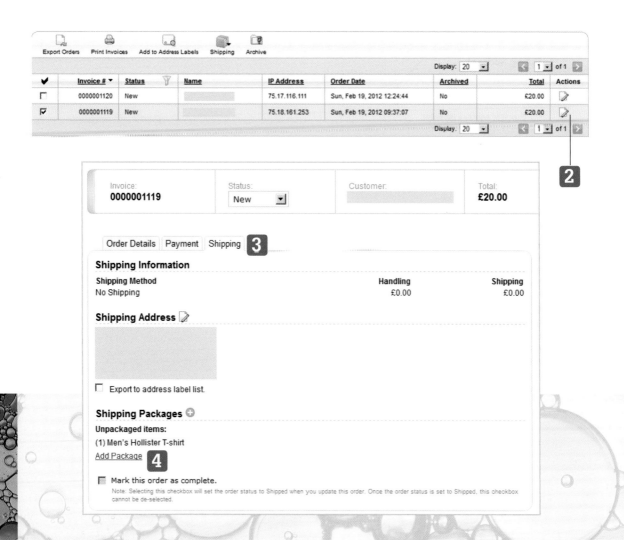

5 Enter a quantity (1, 2, 3 etc.).

6 Click OK.

New Package - Invoice #0000001119		☒

Item	Qty ordered	Qty to package
Men's Hollister T-shirt	1	1 **5**

6 OK   Cancel

HOT TIP: Consider adding a business card or note with your store's logo to the package.

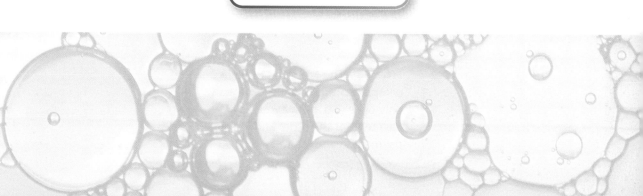

Complete the order and enter shipping information

It's important to keep track of orders for your recordkeeping. Follow the steps below to ensure that your store's records are accurate and you don't have any outstanding issues. It may seem like quite a few steps to complete for one order but it will become much easier the more experience you have with processing and posting your items.

1 Click the Manage menu and select Open Orders.

2 Click the Edit icon.

3 Click the Shipping tab.

4 Enter the Tracking Number (if you have one). **3**

5 Enter the date you shipped (or plan to ship).

6 Click Mark this order as complete.

Order Details   Payment   Shipping

Shipping Information

Shipping Method	Handling	Shipping
No Shipping	£0.00	£0.00

Shipping Address ✎

David Todd
19375 Calle de Barcelona
Cupertino, CA 95014

☐ Export to address label list.

Shipping Packages ⊕

Package 1	✎⊗
(1) Men's Hollister Long-sleeve T-shirt	**2**

Tracking Number:

4

Ship Date:

5   **6**

☐ Mark this order as complete.
Note: Selecting this checkbox will set the order status to Shipped when you update this order. Once the order status is set to Shipped, this checkbox cannot be de-selected.

OK   Cancel

! ALERT: The Mark this order as complete option will become active only once you accept your PayPal payment for the order and log the payment in your store.

Send your customer a message

Let your customer know when you send their item. Tracking information you entered into the Shipping section will be automatically entered into the email note your customer receives.

From your Quick Shopping Cart page.

1 Click the Manage menu and select Open Orders.

2 Click the Edit icon.

3 Enter order notes if you wish.

4 Click Send Email and select Shipment Status.

5 Select the package number and click OK.

ALERT: An automatic email will be generated and sent to the customer with the basic details of their order. If you want to add any information, you must enter it into the Order Notes before you select Shipment Status.

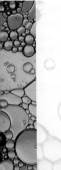

Mark the order as shipped

Your order will continue to appear as 'new' in your Store Summary at the top of your Quick Shopping Cart home page until you mark it as shipped (even though you have probably already shipped the item).

1 Click on Manage and select Orders.

2 Tick the order you want to process.

3 Point your cursor at the shipping icon and select Mark as Shipped.

4 Click OK on the order confirmation screen.

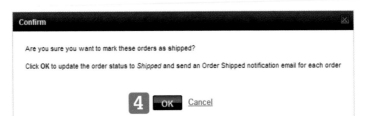

HOT TIP: Consider printing out a copy of the invoice and order summary for your records (though one will be kept electronically on your site).

Manage unique or non-inventoried items

Up until now, we haven't looked at how to keep track of inventory in your store front. If you have one-of-a-kind items for sale in your shop, once they sell you need to make sure that they are no longer displayed on your store front. You need to do this manually through the Manage Products menu at the top of the Quick Shopping Cart. You can also inventory these items, and others, which we will explore in the next section.

1 Click on the Manage menu and select Products.

2 Click in the tick box next to the item that has sold.

3 Click the red delete icon.

Add Product	Price	Import/Export	Featured	Hide	Inventory	Settings	Category	Options	Cross-Sells	Up-Sells	Delete

Display: 20 ▾   ◄ 1 ▾ of 1 ►

✔	Title ▲	Part # (SKU)	Type	List Price	Cur. Sale Price	Inventory	Manufacturer	Featured	Hidden	Actions
☐	Muscle T-shirt	804154166	Standard	£11.00	No	No	Abercrombie & Fitch	No	No	
☑	Men's Hollister Long-sleeve T-shirt	603657706	Standard	£20.00	N/A	N/A	No Manufacturer	No	No	

2

3

! ALERT: Until you delete the selection for a non-inventoried item, it will continue to show in your store front.

Inventory your store items

Whether you sell a number of similar items or ones that are all very different, you want to keep track of them so that your store doesn't display items you don't have in stock. You need to go through each of your product pages and check they are inventoried. After going through these steps, you will be updated when inventory is low or out.

1 Go to the Manage menu and select Products.

2 Tick a product to inventory and click the Edit button.

3 Select Yes next to Inventoried.

4 Enter a number next to Quantity In Stock.

5 Choose when to be notified when stock is low.

6 Scroll to the bottom of the page and click OK.

⊟ **Product**

* Required

Product Type: ◉ **Standalone:** Product with one SKU and no variations. ❷

Part Number (SKU): * `603604954` ❷

Inventoried: ○ No ◉ Yes ❷ **3**

Allow Backorder: ○ Yes ◉ No

Quantity In Stock: * `0` **4**

Email Me When Stock Is: * `0` **5**

Charge for Shipping: ○ Yes ◉ No ❷

International Shipping: You have enabled International Shipping to specific countries. Exclude specific countries for this product. ❷

○ **Configurable Variations:** Product with a unique SKU for each option. ❷

○ **Bundle:** Combination of standalone products into a bundle with one price. ❷

○ **Downloadable:** Digitally downloadable product. ❷

HOT TIP: Decide when to receive a low stock notice by thinking about how long an order from your wholesaler or manufacturer usually takes.

DID YOU KNOW? After you inventory your items, you can manage them through the Manage Inventory section of the Quick Shipping Cart menu.

Issue a refund

If you have a return policy and for some reason your customer returns the item, you will need to refund their money via PayPal. It's a good idea to have a refund policy on certain items (non-perishables, etc.). Larger websites regularly offer these sorts of refund policies and to stay competitive, you should too.

1 Log into your PayPal account.

2 Click on Payments received.

3 Select Issue Refund.

4 Enter the refund amount and invoice number.

5 Add a note to the buyer.

6 Click Continue and process the refund.

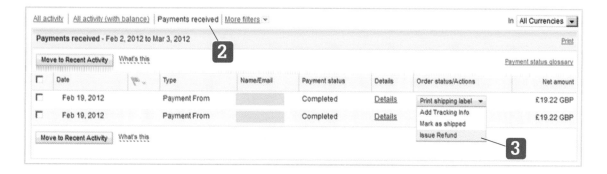

ALERT: You will be refunded a portion of the PayPal fee for the refund but PayPal keeps the fixed-portion fee of your transaction. Check your PayPal account details to see what the fixed-portion fee is for your account.

6 Promote your business

Introduction

While you already have a website up and running and may have sold a few items, you need to devote some time to creating new customers and learning how to keep them coming back. You can do this by tempting them with special offers and also through search engine optimisation (SEO). Search engines are the backbone of the Internet and understanding how people use them will help you attract customers to your site. Note that some of the topics in this chapter, such as SEO, keyword searches and website analytics, are big topics worthy of books in their own right. What you get in this chapter is an introduction to them and information on the basic tools you need to get started with these essential marketing tools.

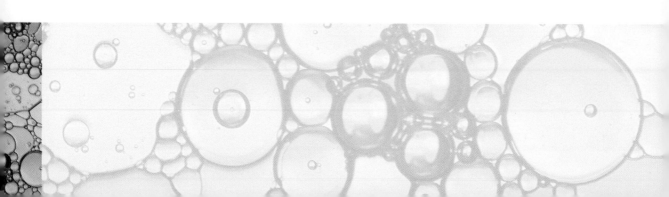

Create a special offer

One way to attract customers and to keep existing customers coming back is to promote your site through a special offer or promotion. The words 'free' and 'discount' do wonders for generating interest in your business, with both new and existing customers. Some offer types include:

- 20 per cent off when the customer registers and buys their first item
- free shipping when the customer registers with your site
- free information (e.g. if you sell gardening supplies, write a booklet on garden maintenance)
- free estimate (if you offer a service).

? DID YOU KNOW?

Most website-building packages come with promotional tools built into them. Check with your provider for details on special offers you can create on your site.

Create a coupon code

A coupon through your website is much like a coupon you use in a shop, redeemed at the time of purchase. When a customer places an order, there is a box where they can enter a coupon code (a simple series of letters or numbers) and receive a discount on their order. You can vary offers and let your existing customers know about them through email.

1 Click on the Promote menu and select Add Coupon.

2 Type in a short coupon code (FREESHIP, 15Off, etc.).

3 Enter a description.

4 Limit the dates and number of uses if you wish.

5 Select a discount type from the drop-down menu (Amount, Percent, Free Shipping & Handling).

6 Enter a Discount percent value (if applicable).

7 Click OK.

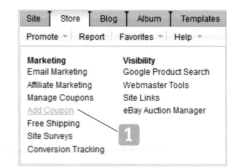

HOT TIP: Consider limiting the number of times an individual customer can use a discount as well as limiting the discount period.

ALERT: When you make changes to your site, click Publish to update the new information to your page.

Keep in contact with your customers

If you have a list of customers from either your bricks-and-mortar shop or from your online one, make sure that you keep them up to date with any changes, additions or special offers you are promoting. You want to create repeat customers and also encourage them to share information about you with their friends and family (your future customers).

- Send a follow-up note a few weeks after a customer buys something to check they are happy or let them know about a related product they may be interested in.
- Let them know about any special offers.
- Send information about new products.
- Update them with changes to your website (e.g. adding an information section or blog).

ALERT: Don't bombard your customers with emails. Schedule a regular email newsletter, perhaps once or twice a month or when you have something new in stock or run a promotion.

DID YOU KNOW?
If anyone asks not to receive emails from your business you must, by law, honour the request and remove them from your mailing list.

Understand SEO

Search engine optimisation (SEO) is the process of getting your website listed in search engine results for specific keywords. For example, if you have an organic skincare business, you want your website displayed near the top of the search results when a consumer searches for 'organic skincare'. Search engines such as Google, Yahoo! and Bing base their rankings in part on the keywords their computers find on the millions of websites they analyse. In fact, their computers (called crawlers, bots or spiders) trawl through the Internet looking for websites – you don't have to do anything to be found by them. Some key points about SEO include the following:

- Find the best keywords for your business (see next section).
- Embed the relevant keywords within your site to get the search engines to find them.
- Have your site linked from other sites (called inbound links).
- Update and change your content often (a static site with little change in content will rank lower in the results).

HOT TIP: Reach out to other businesses, blogs or websites of friends who may have an interest in linking your website with theirs. Inbound links affect how your site is ranked in the results (the more links, the better).

DID YOU KNOW?
Adding a blog or an information section to your website and updating it frequently is a good way to add dynamic content to your site.

Define your keywords for search engines

You need to learn what keywords consumers use to find the types of services or products that you offer on your site. There are keyword suggestion tools you can pay for, but Google offers one for free that will help you define the best keywords to use on your website.

1 Go to adwords.google.co.uk

2 Click Get keyword ideas.

3 Enter the keyword or words that relate closely to your business.

4 Enter the distorted words shown and click Search.

Product surve

Find keywords
Based on one or more of the following:

Word or phrase	
Website	www.google.com/page.html
Category	Apparel

☐ Only show ideas closely related to my search terms ⑦

⊞ Advanced Options and Filters | Locations: United Kingdom ✖ | Languages: English ✖ | Devices: Desktops and laptops

Type the characters that appear in the picture below.
Or sign in to get more keyword ideas tailored to your account. ⑦

Mercury,

Letters are not case-sensitive

Search

About this data ⑦

HOT TIP: Do more than one keyword search. After you get some keyword ideas, enter those into the keyword ideas tool and see whether or not you get more relevant results.

5 Look at other keywords with high values that relate to your business.

Keyword ideas (100)			
Keyword	Competition	Global Monthly Searches ⑦	Local Monthly Searches ⑦
☆ organic skin care brands	High	1,900	210
☆ natural organic skin care	High	3,600	720
☆ skin care products	High	301,000	27,100
☆ natural skin care products	High	18,100	2,400
☆ organic skin care reviews	High	1,600	170
☆ 100 organic skin care	High	390	73
☆ organic skin care products	High	12,100	1,300
☆ skin care organic	High	60,500	9,900
☆ organic baby skin care	High	1,000	170
☆ organic skin care uk	High	1,000	720
☆ organic skin products	High	12,100	1,600
☆ skin care cream	High	60,500	6,600
☆ paraben free skin care	High	1,300	260
☆ discount skin care	Medium	5,400	1,300
☆ skin care natural products	High	18,100	2,400
☆ certified organic skin care	High	1,600	140
☆ skin care natural	High	74,000	9,900
☆ beauty skin care	High	49,500	5,400

Add keywords to your website

Add keywords to your product titles and product descriptions to make it easy for search engines to find and rank your store in the results. Some website builders may have a dedicated section where you can enter these keywords. If they don't, you have to enter them manually into your product and category pages. Remember to enter them into your site's slogan at the top of your page as well.

1 Click Manage and select Products.

2 Click on one product.

3 Scroll down and click the SEO tab.

4 Enter keywords into the Meta Tag Title section and the Description section.

5 Click OK.

6 Repeat the process for categories.

ALERT: Bear in mind that keywords are not the only factor in optimising your search results. You still need to create new and interesting content and continue to develop inbound links to your site.

⊞ Category:

⊞ Images:

⊟ Search Engine Optimization (SEO):

Meta Tag Title:

Meta Tag Description:
(300 characters)

Meta Tag Keywords:
(1,000 characters)

⊞ Attributes:

⊞ Options:

⊞ Up-Sells and Cross-Sells:

5 OK

ALERT: Avoid the temptation to include popular keywords that don't relate to your business. Padding your website with these unrelated keywords is known as keyword spamming and is considered bad practice.

HOT TIP: When you create written content for your site, whether the longer product descriptions or perhaps a blog, be sure to use those keywords you identified as relevant whenever possible.

Understand website analytics

Website analytic tools help you keep track of the visitors on your site and can tell you things such as how many 'hits' your site has had, how visitors found you and whether those visitors were new or returning. It can also tell you about things like conversions and bounces, vital information to any web marketing campaign. Conversion is the goal of SEO: you want to convert a hit, or visit, into a purchase. Tracking conversions (and bounces) is a useful way to gauge whether or not the content on your site is helping your business.

- Go to www.google.com/analytics/index.html and sign up for the free tool.
- Check with your service provider about how to incorporate the code into your site.
- Monitor your site traffic after launching a new promotion or marketing campaign to see whether or not they increased conversion.

HOT TIP: Website analytics are sometimes referred to as site reports by some service providers.

WHAT DOES THIS MEAN?

Bounce: when your site receives a hit but the visitor spends very little time before leaving it again.

? DID YOU KNOW?

The analytics tool is simply a section of code (letters and numbers) that you copy and paste into your website. Most website builders, including Go Daddy, have a location on the site builder where you can paste the code.

Use free advertising credits

Many site-building companies offer newly registered businesses credits to advertise their website on the main search engines and social networking sites. Paying for advertising will display your webpage when consumers do a search for specific keywords. Go Daddy offers credits for Google, Facebook and Yahoo!/Bing, and your site builder may, too. Take advantage of these credits and track whether or not the ads make a difference for your business. If they do, you may want to invest in a paid advertising strategy for your website.

1 Log into your Go Daddy account and click My Account.

2 Scroll down to Free Advertising Credits and click Learn More.

3 Click Activate Credit next to the advertising option you want to try first.

4 Follow the steps to use the credit with your site.

Advertisement Credits

Return to My Account

Advertisement Credits

Whether your goal is to drive traffic to your site or advertise your product or service, advertisement credits make it easy to reach potential customers already searching the 'Net for information about your products and services. Note: It may take up to an hour to receive your ad credit, after an eligible purchase.

Ad Credit Partner	Credit Amount	Order ID	Credit Status	Credit Details
bing | YAHOO! SEARCH	$50	392258282	Activate Credit	Not Activated
facebook	$50	392258282	Activate Credit **3**	Not Activated
Google	$100	392258282	Activate Credit	Not Activated

? DID YOU KNOW?

Paid ad results display differently from natural search results. They are usually shown in highlighted boxes or to the right of the natural search results.

Create a Facebook page

Facebook is a social media tool where people connect with their friends, business colleagues and post about their daily lives and favourite things. It has become an increasingly relevant tool for small businesses to let customers know about their latest product lines, services and any other special offers they want to promote. Once you create a page, encourage customers (or even your friends and relatives) to 'like' your page.

- Go to www.facebook.com/business
- Create a page highlighting your products or services.
- Create special offers available only on Facebook.
- Let your customers know they can receive special offers there.

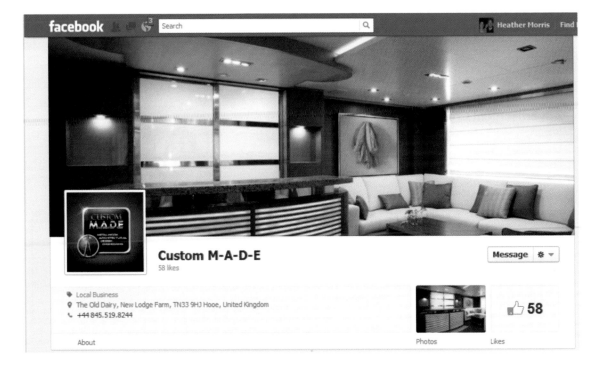

HOT TIP: You can also pay for advertisements to be displayed on individual users' Facebook pages. Use any advertising credit you get with your web-building package to try this out.

ALERT: When you create your Facebook page, be sure to have a link to your main webpage.

Use Pinterest

Pinterest is a popular social media tool that has many applications for small businesses. Pinterest allows individual users to create visual boards or a collection of images they like and find either interesting or inspiring. The images that make up the board are linked to webpages. If a customer 'pins' an image from your site on to their board, their friends or followers can click on the image and be taken to your page. You can encourage customers to pin your site images to their boards by creating a competition or promotion.

Some things to keep in mind about Pinterest:

- Sign up for Pinterest through Facebook or Twitter or get an invitation from a friend on Pinterest.
- Send a request to join if you don't have a Twitter or Facebook account.
- Copy a 'Pin it' button to your website so customers can share your site.
- Encourage customers to pin images they like on your site.
- Create your own board on Pinterest that features a few of your products.

ALERT: Pinterest prohibits direct advertising on its site but companies can create boards that features items related to their business. See Pinterest.com for more information on the policies for small business.

? DID YOU KNOW?
Pinterest generates more small business referrals than either Facebook or Google.

7 Explore other payment options and online security

Introduction

As your business grows you may want to offer your customers more ways to buy from your website or change the way you process payments. This chapter will look at other types of payment options offered by online payment systems such as PayPal and also whether or not an Internet merchant account (IMA) might make sense for your business. Whatever payment options you decide on, you want to make sure that you do all you can to secure your online business. Steps for protecting your business data and that of your customers will be explored as well.

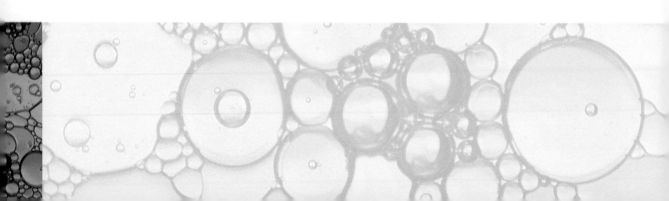

Explore PayPal options

To get your online business up and running quickly, you probably signed up with PayPal to process transactions from your website. PayPal works with several e-commerce building sites, including Actinic, Go Daddy and Moonfruit, to offer payment options within the site. The basic option, called Website Payment Standards, is fine when you are starting up and allows you to quickly accept credit cards on your site. However, once your business is more established, you may want to add other PayPal options to your site to offer your customers more choice.

- Website Payments Pro – you can accept credit card payments directly on your website without a merchant account.
- Express Checkout – customers who choose to complete their purchase with PayPal can do so in three clicks.
- Virtual Terminal – you can process a customer's payment by phone or post. You enter the information into PayPal to make it simpler for the customer.

HOT TIP: Using PayPal to process credit card payments for your business is a good option if you are not ready to sign up for an Internet merchant account.

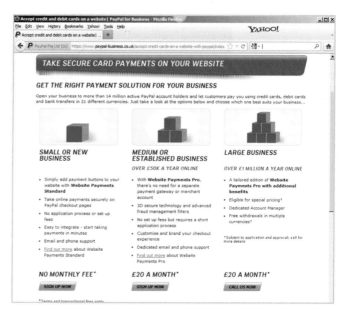

? DID YOU KNOW?
With the Website Payments Pro option you also get Express Checkout and Virtual Terminal or you can use either one alone.

HOT TIP: Check with your e-commerce provider to see about changing or upgrading your PayPal account.

Consider setting up an Internet merchant account (IMA)

In order to process credit and debit card payments without a service such as PayPal, you need to open an IMA with an aquiring bank. If you have a merchant account because you have an existing bricks-and-mortar shop, you will have to open a separate merchant account for online payments. Consider opening an IMA once your business is more established and you want to have payments going directly to you rather than waiting for them to be processed by a payment-processing company.

- Compare rates at different banks and ask about the fees involved in setting up a merchant account and about how long the application process takes (see www.electronic-payments.co.uk/acquiring_banks.jsp).
- Check whether or not your website builder has a preferred bank for merchant accounts and you can get a discount by using them.
- Focus on banks that specialise in providing merchant accounts to online businesses.

? DID YOU KNOW?

A number of larger banks such as HSBC, Alliance and Leicester and Bank of Scotland are acquiring banks and can open an Internet merchant account for you. There is usually a set-up fee as well as a fee per transaction.

! ALERT: It can take up to a month or longer to set up a merchant account if you are a new business. Prepare your business details in advance, including your business plan and details of your accounts.

Learn about SSL security certificates

After you have an Internet merchant account set up, you will need a Secure Sockets Layer (SSL) certificate for your site to protect your customers' credit details and personal information. These certificates encrypt information transmitted over the Internet so that sensitive data, such as credit card details, can't be intercepted by a third party. You have to pay an extra fee to enable this feature on your site.

- Have an approved merchant account set up.
- Check whether or not the website-building company you are using offers this service.
- Compare set-up fees of different SSL certificate providers.

? DID YOU KNOW?

Once you have a security certificate, when your customers shop on your site they'll see a padlock symbol in the URL and the prefix changes to https: to show the site is secure.

! ALERT: You don't have to buy a security certificate if you are using a service such as PayPal, which encrypts customers' data safely. However, some business analysts believe offering this to your customers is likely to attract customers who wouldn't otherwise shop on the Internet.

Protect your business information on a shared computer

Ideally, you will have a computer in your home office exclusively dedicated to your business. However, when you start out you may find yourself sharing this valued resource with others in your household. Be aware that other users can inadvertently move or even delete important files and there are steps you should take to protect your business. You can set up a separate user account for others to use and also add a password to protect your user account so that nobody else will access it.

To create a new user account:

1 From the Start menu select Control Panel and then User Accounts.

2 Click Manage another account and click Create a new account.

3 Enter a user account name next to Standard user.

4 Click Create Account.

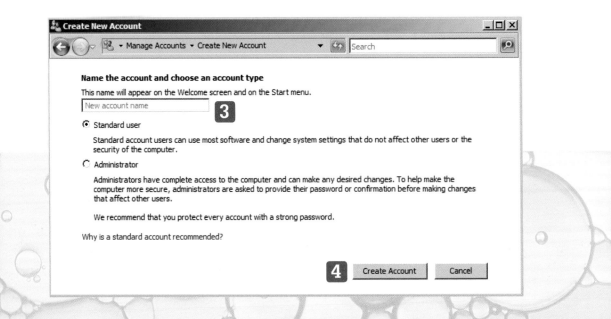

5 Click the Start menu and select Switch user from the menu.

To add a password to your user account:

6 Return to User Accounts and click Create a password for your account.

7 Enter your password twice, create a hint and click Create password.

Create Your Password — ☐ ☒

← → ▾ 🗐 ▾ Create Your Password ▾ 🔁 Search 🔍

Create a password for your account

Dave and Heather
Administrator

New password

Confirm new password

If your password contains capital letters, they must be typed the same way every time you log on.
How to create a strong password

Type a password hint **7**

The password hint will be visible to everyone who uses this computer.
What is a password hint?

Create password   Cancel

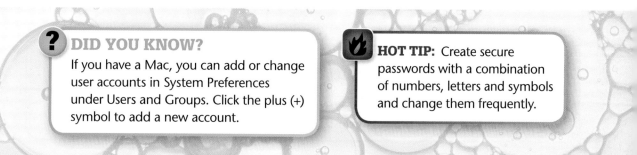

? DID YOU KNOW?
If you have a Mac, you can add or change user accounts in System Preferences under Users and Groups. Click the plus (+) symbol to add a new account.

🔥 HOT TIP: Create secure passwords with a combination of numbers, letters and symbols and change them frequently.

Protect your computer against viruses and malware

PCs and Macs are both vulnerable to malicious software that you may accidentally download through email messages or while using the Internet. If you don't already have a strategy in place to protect your computer from viruses and other types of malware, consider buying an anti-virus program to keep your business data safe.

- Download a free trial of an anti-virus program at http://download.cnet.com
- Consider investing in a well-known anti-virus program such as McAfee or Symantec Anti-virus.
- Keep your anti-virus program up to date. Security software developers regularly come up with new ways to protect your computer against malware.
- Update your browser software when updates are available as these updates contain security fixes to help protect you on the Internet.

HOT TIP: You can further protect your computer from malicious software by not opening attachments from unknown senders.

WHAT DOES THIS MEAN?

Virus: a type of malware, though the two terms are often interchanged.

Malware: the overall term for malicious software that can damage your data or tap into your personal information. Though most programs to protect your computer are called anti-virus programs, most good ones protect against a range of threats.

Use wireless Internet connections safely

Many homes now connect to the Internet wirelessly through a router supplied by a broadband provider. Wireless networks can fall victim to hackers trying to tap into computers on the network or trying to use the network themselves. There are several steps you can take to protect your computer and business data from would-be thieves.

- Create a strong password to protect your wireless router.
- Consider setting up a virtual private network (VPN) on your home business wireless network.
- Turn off file sharing in public Wi-Fi spots or avoid using free, public Wi-Fi spots with your work laptop.
- Consider using a software firewall on your computer.

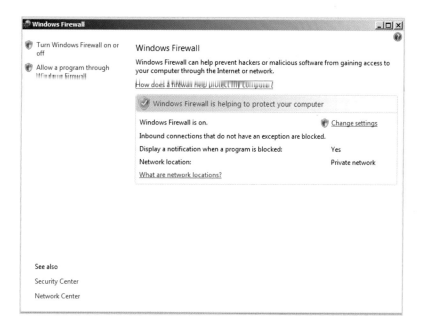

WHAT DOES THIS MEAN?
Firewall: protects you from hackers trying to access your computer through a network connection.

HOT TIP: A strong password should consist of more than ten characters and a combination of letters, numbers, symbols and mixed cases.

Back up your business data

Computers can crash and lose information for any number of reasons, not all of which are possible to anticipate. To protect your business, back up the following kinds of data: your accounts, any contact information for your customers and product information or images. Think about important data in terms of how your business would be affected if you lost that information on your computer.

1 Go to the Start menu and select Control Panel.

2 Click Backup and Restore.

3 Click Back up files.

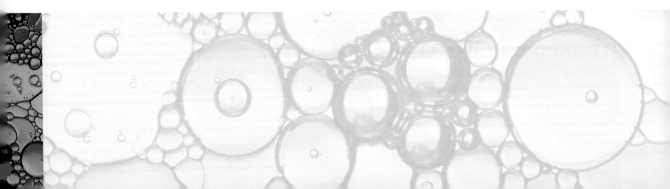

4 Select a backup location (external hard drive, disk, etc.) and click Next.

5 Select disks to include in the backup and click Next.

6 Tick the types of files you want to back up and click Next.

7 Click Save settings and start backup.

Back Up Files ✕

Back Up Files

Where do you want to save your backup?

⦿ On a hard disk, CD, or DVD:

My Book (J:) 149.6 GB free ▾ **4**

○ On a network:

Browse...

Why don't I see my hard disk?

What's the difference between backing up files and copying files to a CD?

4 Next Cancel

HOT TIP: Invest in an external hard drive for regular backups, but consider backing up your data to disks (CD or DVD) as well, and store the disks away from your computer and office.

8 Sell on eBay

Introduction

eBay offers a one-stop website for millions of sellers and buyers worldwide. You can open another sales channel for your business by listing some of your products on ebay.co.uk, too. You may not want to sell everything that you sell on your website on eBay so check around first and see whether or not there is potential for you to market your product competitively. In the past few years eBay has become less of an auction site and there is a tendency towards more fixed-price buying, which offers great opportunities for businesses. You don't have to leave your items up for auction but you do have to be competitive with other sellers. This chapter will outline the basics of selling on eBay, but bear in mind there is more that won't be covered, such as setting up an eBay store or becoming a power seller, which are things you should consider doing down the line if you feel that eBay is a good sales venue for your business.

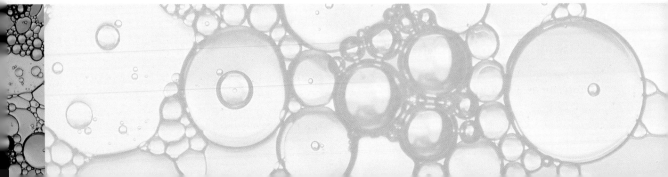

Understand eBay business basics

As an eBay business, you can choose either fixed-price or auction-style listings as you would with an individual account. When you register as a business on the site you need to provide valid contact details as well as details of a bank account that can accept direct debit instructions. If you are registered for VAT, you'll provide your VAT registration number to set up your business account. Other eBay business basics to keep in mind include the following:

- You can't sell your business goods as an individual – you must register for a business account.
- You pay a lower listing fee as a business but you still have to pay a final-value fee if your item sells.
- You are subject to the same feedback rating system as individual sellers and must strive to provide good customer service to earn positive feedback.
- There are several types of shop you can open up as a business, for which you pay a monthly fee.

SEE ALSO: Go to ebay.co.uk/businesscentre/index.html for more information on how to register as a business.

HOT TIP: You don't have to make use of the shop service but there are advantages to going down this route, including discounts on your listing fees. After you spend a few months selling on eBay, consider investing the £14.99 a month in an eBay shop.

Research completed BIN and auction listings

To get an idea of whether your item will sell better as a fixed-price or Buy It Now (BIN) item or in an auction, search through completed listings for these different types of pricing strategies. Do a search for the item as a buyer would and use the Advanced search feature to sort your results. This should give you an idea of the demand for an item and also a rough idea of what buyers are willing to pay.

1 Click Advanced next to the Search button on eBay's home page.

2 Enter a keyword.

3 Tick the box for Completed listings.

4 Select a buying format (Auction or Buy It Now).

5 Select a location preference if you wish.

6 Click Search and review the final price for items.

7 Repeat the steps above for a different buying format (e.g. if you chose Buy It Now, try a search by auction).

Location

☑ Only show items:

○ From preferred locations | on eBay UK ▼ | 5

○ Located in | United Kingdom ▼ |

● Available to | United Kingdom ▼ |

Learn more

Currency

| Pound Sterling ▼ |

! ALERT: You may see some results with the final amount in red – this means the item didn't sell. Green numbers are those that have sold and the final price you see is what was paid for the item.

? DID YOU KNOW?
You can do an advanced search with other variables such as whether or not the postage and packaging was free, when the item sold, as well as information on international sales.

Understand eBay sellers' fees

You get a huge potential market for your business on this website but you do have to pay to list your items for sale. There are fees to list your item (insertion fees) as well as fees when the item sells (final-value fees). You pay final-value fees only if your item sells. The fees outlined below are recent at the time of writing. Check with eBay for any updates or changes to the fee structure.

- Auction-style insertion fees for a business seller range from £.10 to £1.30 and depend on the starting price. A lower starting of £.99 will cost £.10 to insert. Media (books, DVDs, music and video games) are only £.05.

- Fixed-price insertion fees vary depending on whether or not you have an eBay shop. Without a shop, you pay a flat rate of £.40 per listing. Shop owners pay from zero to £.10 per listing. Media fees are up to £.20, depending on the type of shop you have.

- Final-value fees apply to both auction and fixed-price listings and depend on the type of category but range from 3 per cent to 12 per cent, depending on the item. See the table for details.

Category	Final value fee
All categories (except those below and vehicles)	10%
Tech	3%
Parts	8%
Media	9%
Collectables	10%
Clothing, shoes and accessories	12%
Property	No fee

HOT TIP: Go to pulse.ebay. co.uk to see what the most popular items have been for that day.

? DID YOU KNOW?

Shop owners get a red shop icon to display on their listings. Interested customers can click on the icon and are taken to the shop to view additional items for sale.

Decide on a pricing and listing strategy

As a business, it's good to bear in mind that people typically come to eBay to get a bargain. Setting an auction will create the sense in potential buyers that they will get a good deal and if there is plenty of interest in the item, you should get a fair price. Note that fees for fixed-price listings tend to be more expensive than for auction listings (especially those with a low starting bid). You can opt to list the item for three, seven or more days with the following formats:

- Auction format: you set a starting bid amount and wait for buyers to place competitive bids.
- Buy It Now: you decide on a price based on your market research. Buyers purchase the item by clicking the Buy It Now button.
- Combined Buy It Now and auction listing: you enter a starting bid and also a Buy It Now price. Once a bid is placed, the BIN option disappears and the item sells at the end of the auction period.

Choose how you'd like to sell your item   Add or remove options | Get help

Get ideas about pricing by searching completed listings.

| Online auction | Fixed price |

ℹ️ List an Online Auction for free. Learn more.

⭐ Starting price (see listing fees) ⑦ Buy It Now price (see listing fees) ⑦

£ 12.99   £ 21.00

No reserve price set for this item. Change

⭐ Quantity

1   item

Duration ⑦

7 days ▾

Private listing ⑦

☐ Allow buyers to remain anonymous to other eBay members

⦿ Start listing immediately

◯ Schedule start time (£0.05) [- ▾] [01 ▾] [00 ▾] GMT

? DID YOU KNOW?

If you have an item that is particularly valuable, you can set a reserve price on your auction. The reserve price will not be seen by customers and your item won't sell if the reserve price isn't met.

🔥 HOT TIP: Beginning with a starting price of £.99 can generate interest in your item as well as increase awareness of your store and of the other items you have for sale.

Create a listing

Before you start, make sure you have a detailed product description and photographs ready to go from your website. If you need help with this, revisit Chapter 2 for tips on how to create these. In general, the listing process on eBay is fairly straightforward.

1 Click Sell on the top of the ebay.co.uk page.

2 Enter a category into the search box and hit return.

3 Tick an appropriate category and click Continue.

4 Enter a listing title, condition and other item specifics as relevant.

ALERT: If you have multiple items that are similar, use the multiple variation listing tool when prompted.

SEE ALSO: See the next section for information on writing an effective title for your listing.

Write a title

You get less than 60 characters to catch a buyer's attention with your title. Do some preliminary searches in the completed listings to see how items were listed. Use the following tips when creating a title for your listing:

- Use keywords rather than whole sentences.
- Use words that describe the specifics of the item (large, red, size 12, etc.).
- Avoid using all capital letters in the title.
- Avoid punctuation and stars * or other symbols.

? DID YOU KNOW?

Many sellers use acronyms in titles. You can use them, but remember that there are new buyers who may be unaware of their meaning. Common acronyms include NWT (new with tags), NIP (new in package), VGC (very good condition, especially for used items), HTF (hard to find).

! ALERT: Avoid keyword spamming in your title and product description. Some sellers list a number of other related items in the title to catch the attention of buyers. This is strictly prohibited on eBay.

Add photographs

Images are one of your best selling tools online. With eBay you can upload more than one image to your listing. Take advantage of this and display different shots of your product, perhaps of a small or noteworthy detail or from different angles. See Chapter 2 for information on taking an effective photograph of your products.

1 Click Add Pictures.

2 Click Browse to find images on your computer that you want to use.

3 Adjust the brightness or crop images with the tools on the right.

4 Click Upload.

Write an item description and set a price

Use your saved descriptions of your item from your e-commerce site. Open the Word or text document and copy the descriptions into the eBay page. You shouldn't need to edit them too much.

1 Type or copy and paste your product description from your existing website.

2 Choose a font type and style.

3 Consider adding a theme with the Listing designer.

4 For an auction, enter a starting bid.

5 Click the Fixed price tab and enter an amount if you want a BIN listing.

6 Choose a sale duration and/or schedule a start time.

HOT TIP: In general, the busiest shopping days on eBay are Sundays and Mondays, so consider ending your auction then. The market for your product may be slightly different so you can experiment with ending days and times to find the best ones for your market.

ALERT: You will be charged an additional fee if you schedule a start time for your auction.

Choose payment options

Many eBay customers will use PayPal but some newer users may not. Consider whether or not your potential customers would benefit from including other payment options such as payment by postal order or personal cheque.

1 Enter your PayPal address.

2 Tick Require immediate payment when buyer uses Buy it now (if you wish).

3 Select other payment options.

ALERT: Some buyers who use the BIN option are not aware of how to complete all the steps to pay for their item. If you require immediate payment for these items, your customer will be prompted through the steps to complete their purchase.

Select postage options

Buyers generally like to know how much postage is before they bid on or buy something. You can add any cost on top of the postage fee. For example, if the average amount of postage is £2.50, you can add the cost of the envelope on top of that and make the total postage £3. Check out what other businesses are charging for postage and stay competitive with them. Take time to measure and weigh your item so that you can use the calculated postage option.

If you are a new seller, you may have to select a fixed postage price.

1 Decide whether you will do estimated or flat rate.

2 Tick if OK to pick up.

3 Consider P&P discounts.

4 Select dispatch time.

Firefox ▾

eBay > Create your listing   ×   My eBay Account: Addresses   ×   +

cgi5.ebay.co.uk/ws/eBayISAPI.dll#lnkLocation   ebay.co.uk

Q ebay.co.uk   SEARCH

Give buyers P&P details   Add or remove options | Get help

* Domestic postage
Flat Same cost to all buyers   **1**
Services   Postage Estimator   Cost
Royal Mail 1st Class Standard (1 to 2 working days)   £ 2.00   ☐ Free P&P
Offer additional service

Local pick up
☐ Buyers can pick up the item from you   **2**

Combined P&P discounts
No combined P&P discount rules have been created.   **3**
Create rules

Dispatch time
Select a dispatch time   **4**

International postage
No international postage
Your item will appear only on eBay UK.

Exclude postage locations
No locations are excluded.
Create exclusion list

Item location
Hastings, East Sussex, TN34 2BH, United Kingdom
Change location

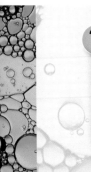

? DID YOU KNOW?
Postage and packing (P&P) discounts offer a lower combined shipping rate to customers who buy more than one product from you.

! ALERT: It is generally a good idea to keep your dispatch time down (1–2 days maximum) to keep customers happy and interested in buying from you again.

Include a returns policy

As a business seller on eBay, you must have a returns policy for your products. Consumers are protected under the Distance Selling Regulations. You must check what your minimum legal obligations are and whether or not your products and listing types fall under the jurisdiction of the Distance Selling Regulations.

1 Click Change under Return policy.

2 Select Returns Accepted.

3 Enter your policy details and click Save.

Other things you'd like buyers to know Add or remove options | Get help

Buyer requirements
Use buyer requirements to block certain buyers from bidding on or purchasing your items.

None: Allow all buyers
Add buyer requirements

*Return policy
• No returns accepted.
Change

Additional check out instructions

Note: 500 character limit

Return Policy

○ Returns Not Accepted

◉ Returns Accepted

Additional return policy details

Note: 5000 character limit.

Save Cancel

HOT TIP: You can require the buyer to pay the postage cost of returning the item if you clearly state this in your listing before the item is purchased.

SEE ALSO: Some of the basics of the types of laws that apply to online transactions are explored in Chapter 10.

Monitor your sales and respond to queries

Over the course of the sale period you can check how many people have viewed your item or are watching it on their eBay page. You may also receive notes from potential buyers which you'll want to respond to right away. Common messages include queries about shipping options and more details about the product than are included in your listing. You should be notified via email when you have a message but you can also check for messages on your eBay Selling page.

1 Point your cursor at My eBay at the top of the page and select Selling.

2 Scroll down to Active selling to monitor any sales or interest.

3 Click on the Messages tab at the top and click on a message.

3

Activity	Messages (2)	Account	Applications NEW

All selling	The My eBay landing page is set to Summary [Change]

Summary

▼ Buy
Bids/Offers (0)
Didn't win (0)
Deleted

▼ Lists
All lists
Watch list & other lists
Saved searches (0)
Saved sellers (0)

Purchase history

▼ Sell
All selling
Scheduled (0)
Active (4)
Sold (1)
Unsold (0)
Postage labels
Deleted

Want to buy from the best?
We help you find them
eBay Top-Rated Sellers
Find out more ▸

Totals   Edit ▾
Selling totals

Selling reminders   Edit ▾
(Last 31 days)
☆ I have 1 active item with questions from buyers.
🐾 1 item I sold is eligible for a Second Chance Offer.

Scheduled (0)   Print | Edit ▾
◂ All (0) ▸

You do not have any scheduled items for sale.

To see a scheduled listing that has started, go to **Active selling**.

Active selling (4) **2**   Print | Edit ▾

◂ All (4) | Awaiting answer (1) | Open offers (0) | Bids/Reserve met (1) | Without bids/Reserve not met (3) | Leads (0) | Pri ▸

Format All ▾   Sort by Time left: ending soonest ▾

			Watchers	Bids	Price	Time left	Actions
☐	🔎	Yankee Candle - 3 Pack SUN AND SAND Car Jar air freshene... **High bidder:** sailorsixteen (544 ⭐)	2	1	£0.99	6d 20h	**Sell similar** More actions ▾
☐	🔎	Yankee Candle - 3 Pack VANILLA LIME Car Jar air freshene...	5	0	£0.99	6d 20h	**Sell similar** More actions ▾
☐	🔎	**Unanswered question** 10 Yankee Candle Tarts including Kiwi Berries Lemon Vanil... **Questions:** 2	2	0	£0.99	6d 21h	**Respond** More actions ▾
☐	🔎	8 Yankee Candle Samplers Votive including Kiwi Berries St...	1	0	£0.99	6d 21h	**Sell similar** More actions ▾

4 Click the yellow Respond tab to reply and type your message.

5 Consider posting the message to the listing page so other potential buyers can see it.

6 Click Send.

Send | Cancel

10 Yankee Candle Tarts including Kiwi Berries Lemon Vanilla Rainforest
Item number: **250984048372**
Price: **£0.99**
Time left: **6d 20h**

To:

Subject: Re: Combined postage: ▮▮▮▮ sent a message about 10 Yankee Candle Tarts including Kiwi Berries Lemon Vanilla Rainforest #250984048372

I'm happy to combine postage, which would be 3.00 for both lots. I'm going to leave the sale an auction but may have other Buy It Now orders in the coming week.

1840 characters left

From:
To:
Subject: Combined postage: sent a message about 10 Yankee Candle Tarts including Kiwi Berries Lemon Vanilla Rainforest #250984048372
Sent Date: 29-Jan-12 21:33:19 GMT

Hi,

☐ Send a copy to my personal email address
☑ Post this question and response on my listing so all buyers can see it. **5**
   Once posted can't be edited

6 Send | Cancel

🔥 **HOT TIP:** Posting the message to your eBay sale page will help other potential buyers.

⚠ **ALERT:** Shill bidding, where you get a friend to bid on an item in order to increase the final price, is prohibited on eBay.

Accept PayPal payment

Once an item sells, you will be notified via the email address you registered with eBay or by checking on your Selling (Sold) items under My eBay. From here on, you will be interacting with the Action menu section on your eBay selling page both to accept payment and to print postage.

1 Click View PayPal transaction.

2 Log into your PayPal account with your password.

3 Click the Overview tab.

4 Click Accept next to the transaction.

5 Click Accept this payment, then click Submit.

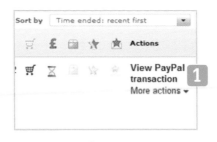

	Date		Type	Name/Email	Payment status	Details	Order status/Actions	Gross
☐	Mar 15, 2012		Payment From		Unclaimed	Details	Accept **4**	£21.49 GBP

My recent activity | Payments received | Payments sent   View all of my transactions

My recent activity - Last 7 days (Mar 8, 2012-Mar 15, 2012)

Archive What's this   Payment status glossary

Archive What's this

? DID YOU KNOW?

The money for both the item and the postage will be transferred to your account. Once you've accepted payment, you can use the funds to buy postage.

Print postage

You can print out postage and any invoice and order details directly from your computer. The print postage option through eBay is available for UK buyers only. You have a few carrier options, including Royal Mail.

1 Click on Print postage label from the Actions menu.

2 Choose a shipping carrier and click Continue.

3 Check the details of the order and enter the package information.

4 Click Continue to purchase and print the postage label.

Period	Last 31 days					Sort by	Time ended: recent first	

			Price	Sale date	🛒	£ 📇 ⭐ ⭐	Actions	
☐	🔧	Men's Abercrombie & Fitch Muscle T-shirt Grey Extra Large	£18.99	15/03/12	🛒	£	Print postage label	**1**
		(27 ☆) 100.0%					More actions ▾	
		Watch count: 3						

! ALERT: If you haven't accepted PayPal payment this option may not be available from the Actions menu.

? DID YOU KNOW?
If you have pop-ups blocked in your browser you must unblock them to print postage. Tick Allow pop-ups to do this.

Use eBay tools to promote your products

There are a few free Web-based tools (and one for a small fee) that make it easier for businesses which are selling in bulk to list and market their products. An individual seller may list only a few items each month whereas a business is likely to list dozens or even hundreds of items for sale. Explore whether or not your business would benefit from one or more of the tools listed below.

- Turbo Lister is free to download from eBay and makes it easier to edit, save and upload information about your product listings. It's a free software program that you download to your desktop (http://pages.ebay.co.uk/turbo_lister).
- Selling Manager helps you keep track of your active listings, generate feedback and also print invoices and labels for your items. You can use the tool without downloading it to your desktop (http://pages.ebay.co.uk/selling_manager).
- Sales Report Overview helps you generate information about your eBay activity to include in any review of your sales. There is a free option and a free trial of Sales Report Plus.

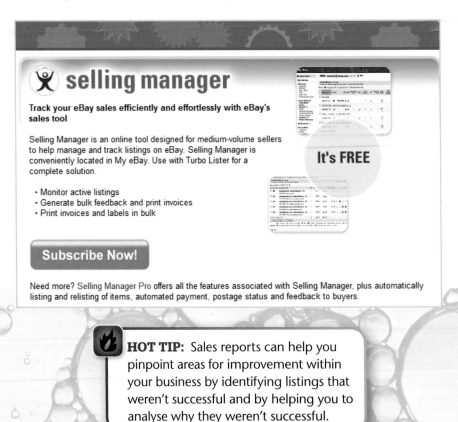

selling manager

Track your eBay sales efficiently and effortlessly with eBay's sales tool

Selling Manager is an online tool designed for medium-volume sellers to help manage and track listings on eBay. Selling Manager is conveniently located in My eBay. Use with Turbo Lister for a complete solution.

- Monitor active listings
- Generate bulk feedback and print invoices
- Print invoices and labels in bulk

It's FREE

Subscribe Now!

Need more? Selling Manager Pro offers all the features associated with Selling Manager, plus automatically listing and relisting of items, automated payment, postage status and feedback to buyers.

HOT TIP: Sales reports can help you pinpoint areas for improvement within your business by identifying listings that weren't successful and by helping you to analyse why they weren't successful.

9 Sell on Amazon

Introduction

Amazon has transformed from an online bookshop into an 'everything' megastore. It sells a huge variety of consumer goods from electronics to clothing, food, cosmetics, office supplies and more. Several years ago it opened up its website to third-party sellers and you can now use Amazon to market and sell products from your business. With millions of shoppers using the site, you have an instant market for your products that you wouldn't otherwise have when you first start a business.

This chapter will show the steps for selling as a Basic seller only, but you'll get information about a Pro-merchant account as well.

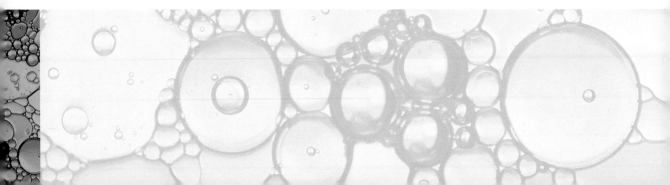

Understand Amazon marketplace

Consumers will see only one listing for any given item but are offered a number of sellers to buy from. Customers use Amazon's secure check-out and their experience of shopping will be the same as it would be if they were buying directly from Amazon. Sellers agree to ship the item within 48 hours of a sale. To see how marketplace listings are displayed, do the following:

1 Search for an item that you stock or some other item from the main search box.

2 Click on the link under More Buying Choices.

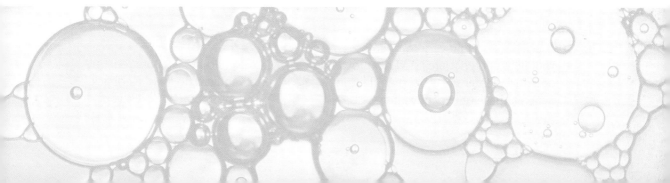

3 Review the price and delivery costs on offer from each marketplace seller.

Price + Delivery	Condition	Seller Information	Buying Options
All 1-15 of 34 offers			

Price + Delivery	Condition	Seller Information	Buying Options
£5.31 + £2.80 delivery	New	Seller: **The Book Depository Ltd** Seller Rating: ★★★★★ **98% positive** over the past 12 months. (2,462,341 total ratings) In stock. Dispatched from United Kingdom. International & domestic delivery rates and return policy. Brand New. Shipped from UK Mainland. Delivery is usually 3 - 4 working days from order by Royal Mail, International Delivery ... » Read more	Add to Basket or Sign in to turn on 1-Click ordering.
£5.32 + £2.80 delivery	New	Seller: **ioub** Seller Rating: ★★★★★ **96% positive** over the past 12 months. (656 total ratings) In stock. Dispatched from United Kingdom. Expedited delivery available. International & domestic delivery rates and return policy. Perfect condition. Despatched via First Class Post/Airmail	Add to Basket or Sign in to turn on 1-Click ordering.
£8.15 & this item **Delivered FREE in the UK** with Super Saver Delivery. See details and conditions Eligible for ✓Prime Learn more	New	amazon.co.uk In stock. Want guaranteed delivery by 1pm Tuesday, March 27? Order it in the next 22 hours and 4 minutes, and choose **Express Delivery** at checkout. See details Domestic delivery rates and return policy.	Add to Basket or Sign in to turn on 1-Click ordering.
£5.56 + £2.80 delivery	New	Seller: **thebumperbook** Seller Rating: ★★★★★ **98% positive** over the past 12 months. (21,484 total ratings) In stock. Dispatched from United Kingdom. Expedited delivery available. Domestic delivery rates and return policy. In Stock, all UK orders despatched SAME WORKING DAY. Items over 25GBP sent via FedEx. Email support for all customers.	Add to Basket or Sign in to turn on 1-Click ordering.

! ALERT: Pricing is very competitive. Your item and price are listed next to potentially dozens of other providers. In general, the least expensive item sells.

? DID YOU KNOW? Customers are encouraged, but not required, to leave feedback on their transaction with you.

Learn about selling options

You gain access to a huge market for your items when selling on Amazon, in return for which you'll incur several fees, including a referral or sales commission fee, a fixed closing fee, and a variable closing fee which Amazon charge for referring the customer to your business, for the sale of the product, and for administering the transaction. The more items you sell, the better your potential for profit margins. You also benefit from offering customers a secure, ready-made check-out and payment system. Selling options include the following:

- Basic seller – if you plan to sell fewer than 35 items per month. You can sell a more limited range of items (see next section) and each item sold will cost £0.75, exclusive of VAT. You can also pay a sales commission to Amazon of 10–15 per cent, depending on the item and a variable closing fee, dependent upon the item category and/or destination.

- Pro seller – if you plan to sell more than 35 items monthly, you will pay a £25 per month fixed fee. You also pay sales commission to Amazon of 7–15 per cent plus a variable closing fee, as above.

WHAT DOES THIS MEAN?
Variable closing fee: this is a fee charged for the administration of the transaction and varies according to the type of item and where the item is being shipped to.

! ALERT: If you are a Basic seller and not VAT registered, the Luxembourg VAT of 15 per cent will be applied to each sale.

Understand what you can sell

What you can sell depends in part on the type of seller account you have. If you list an item with a Basic account, you have far fewer items you can sell. Review the table below for more information about what you can sell.

- Basic sellers can sell only things already in the Amazon catalogue.
- Pro sellers can add items to the Amazon catalogue.
- Certain items must be approved by Amazon before you can sell them.

Basic Seller (fewer than 35 items per month)

Books, DVD, VHS	Musical Instruments & DJ
Computing	Toys & Games
DIY & Tools	Kitchen
Electronics	Sports & Leisure
Software & Video games	
Home & Garden	
Music	

Pro Seller (more than 35 items per month)

All items from Basic seller and:	With approval from Amazon:
Baby	Clothing
Car & Motorbike Parts	Grocery
Lighting	Health & Beauty
Office Products & Supplies	Jewelry
Shoes	Watches
Sports & Leisure	

? DID YOU KNOW?

Items that you can't sell include mobile phones (and mobile services), magazines and newspapers, adult items, tobacco and alcohol, prescription medication and photo processing.

! ALERT: When you sign up to sell on Amazon, your account is set to sell on Amazon in UK, Germany, France, Italy and Spain. You will select your 'home marketplace' when you first sign up.

Sell an item as a Basic seller

Adding an item on Amazon is just a matter of a few clicks and you can start with your existing Amazon account. If you don't have an Amazon account, you can sign up for one with a credit card and your personal details. It's easy to list an item as you can use the existing page as a template to sell.

1 Search for the item in the amazon.co.uk catalogue.

2 Click on the Sell yours here tab beneath the More Buying Choices section on the product page.

More Buying Choices

34 used & new from £5.31

Have one to sell? [Sell yours here] **2**

3 Confirm the product type.

4 Enter the details for your product and the quantity you have for sale.

5 Choose delivery methods, click Continue and complete the listing.

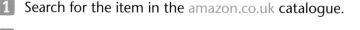

2. Describe the condition of your product:

Choose from the drop-down menu below after reviewing our condition guidelines. Describe the condition of your product accurately to help provide a great buyer experience.

✱ **Condition:** [- Select - ▾]

Condition Note: [ ]
(Add your comments about the condition) Example: Dust cover missing. Some scratches on the front.

3. Enter the price of your product

When your product sells, Amazon charges a fee and a commission in accordance with the participation agreement between you and Amazon. The remainder is deposited in your account. All fees listed above are inclusive of VAT. Learn more about Seller Fees

✱ **Your price:** £ [ ]
(Price based on condition)

4

4. Enter the quantity you have for sale

If you are selling more than one of these products, they must be in the same condition in order to be listed together. If you are selling the product in several different conditions, please repeat this listing process for each condition.

✱ **Quantity:** [1]

5. Select your delivery methods

All sellers are required to offer at least standard delivery. When your product sells, you will receive a shipping credit as shown below. The delivery rates set by Amazon vary by product type. Learn more

Domestic Only:	**Required**
Transit time: 3 - 12 business days	view rate table
Express Delivery - UK:	☐ **Yes**
Transit time: 24 hours	view rate table
International:	[None ▾]
Transit time: 5 - 35 business days	view rate table

5

[Continue]

🔥 **HOT TIP:** If you have the EAN, ISBN or UPC code for the product, you can search for an item using one of those.

🔥 **HOT TIP:** Check competitors' prices and consider offering your item for slightly less, even just a few pence.

Monitor your seller's account

You can monitor your listings through your existing Amazon account. Once you list an item for sale, a seller's account section is automatically added to your Amazon page. To log into the seller's account, do the following from Amazon.co.uk's home page:

1 Sign into your Amazon account.

2 Click Your Account in the upper right corner of the webpage.

3 Click the Your Seller Account link on the right.

4 Click the View your current inventory link beneath Manage Your Inventory.

Your Other Accounts

Your Seller Account **3**
Your Trade-In Account
Corporate Customers
Web Services Account
Amazon Payments Account

[Sell Your Stuff]

Your Orders

In last day:	0
In last 7 days:	0
Pending:	0
Unshipped:	0
Return requests:	0

[View your Orders]

Feedback Rating

★★★★★ **5.0** stars over the past 12 months
(2 ratings)

Feedback	30 days	90 days	365 days
Positive	-	-	100%
Neutral	-	-	0%
Negative	-	-	0%
Count	0	0	2

View your Ratings and Feedback

Other Amazon Links

- Amazon.com Home Page
- Your Buyer Account
- Your Trade-In Account
- Amazon Associates
- Kindle Direct Publishing

Manage Your Inventory
List single items
View your current inventory ——— **4**

Manage Your Orders
View your orders
Issue a refund for an order
Manage returns

Get Paid
View your payments account

Reports
View your performance summary
View your customer metrics summary
View your Ratings and Feedback
Review your A-to-z Guarantee Claims
View your tax document library

Settings
Seller Account Information
Store Settings
Shipping Settings
Amazon.com Settings
Manage returns settings
Notification Preferences

Headlines (see all)

Payments Summary

Recent Payment
Feb 8, 2012 – **9.30**
Disbursed to your bank account ending in

Balance
$0.00

Buyer Messages

Messages without a response:	0
All messages received:	0

In the last 7 days

View your messages

Manage Your Case Log

View your case log

Buyer Claims

A-to-z Guarantee claims:	0
Chargeback claims:	0

Claims requiring action

🔥 **HOT TIP:** Keep an eye on any changes to competitors' pricing in the inventory section. You'll see the lowest price for the item you are selling and can adjust yours if needed.

❓ **DID YOU KNOW?**
This is the main page for you to keep track of all the items you sell on Amazon as well as to check your feedback and respond to messages from buyers.

Post a sold item

You will be notified by email (with the address you have registered with Amazon) that your item has sold. By selling on Amazon, you agree to send out the item within 48 hours of a sale. Do the following to process a sold item:

1. Click on Your Account on the home page and then Your Seller Account.

2. Click View your orders under the Manage Your Orders link.

3. Click Print packing slip and print the details of your order.

4. Buy postage through Amazon if you wish.

	Order Date	Order ID/Product Details	Contact Buyer	Billing Country	Shipping Service	Status	Estimated Delivery	Action
□	Mar 25, 2012 1:42:02 PM PDT	002-3466227-6627462		US	Standard	Unshipped (1)	Mar 30, 2012 to Apr 16, 2012	Print packing slip, Confirm shipment, Buy shipping, Cancel order

Manage Orders Learn more

Make checkout easier. ▸Learn more

Advertisement

Date Range — last 7 days — Search Advanced Search

Total unshipped: 1 order | Total pending: 0 orders

All orders placed in the last 7 day(s) Clear all filters

Orders 1 to 1

Print packing slips for selected orders — GO

Print packing slips for selected orders — GO

HOT TIP: Consider sending out the item within a day if possible to encourage positive buyer feedback.

Confirm shipment

Once you print the packing slip and have postage for the item, possibly including tracking information, you have to confirm shipment. This will generate an email to the customer to let them know their item is on the way. This process should be complete within 48 hours of the sale.

1 Click Your Account and then go to Your Seller Account.

2 Click View your orders.

3 Click Confirm shipment next to the order details.

4 Enter the shipping date.

5 Enter the carrier, shipping service and tracking information if applicable.

6 Click Confirm Shipment.

Confirm shipment Learn more

Fulfillment by Amazon
Let us pack, ship and service your online orders. Learn More | Sign Up

Order ID: # 002-3466227-6627462

Package 1 - UNSHIPPED ITEMS

Product Details	Items to Ship	Items in Package
	1	1 ▾

Order-Item ID: 57721790427722
Condition: Used - Like New

Shipping Details

5

Ship Date:	Carrier:	Shipping Service:	Tracking ID:
Sunday, March 25, 2012 ▾	Select ▾		

4

Confirm shipment **6**

Your notes   Undo   Save

Seller memo:

The information you enter here is for your use only and will not be displayed to the buyer.

! ALERT: It can take 14 days or longer to receive funds in your account. Amazon disburses payment every 14 days but it may take a few days to appear in your account.

? DID YOU KNOW?

You can send the buyer a personal note in the Your notes section of the shipping confirmation page. You can include any special details about the order or simply thank them for their custom.

Register for a Pro seller account

If you find there is a good market for your items on Amazon, you may want to take the plunge and invest in a Pro seller account. This type of account comes with tools (software and Web-based) that help you upload a greater number of products. When you apply, you'll need to have a credit card and your banking details ready as well as your VAT information.

1 Go to Amazon's home page and scroll to the bottom.

2 Click Sell on Amazon.

3 Click Start Selling beneath the Sell a lot tab.

Get to Know Us	Make Money with Us	Let Us Help You
Careers	Sell on Amazon	Delivery Rates & Policies
Investor Relations	Associates Programme	Amazon Prime
Press Releases	Fulfilment by Amazon	Returns Are Easy
Amazon and Our Planet	Self-publish with Us	Manage Your Kindle
	› See all	Help

amazon.co.uk

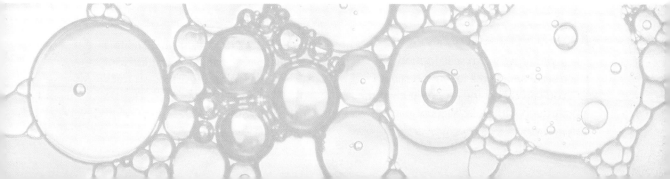

4 Select the Create a new account option.

5 Enter your contact information and click Continue to complete your registration with your bank account and other details.

amazon services
seller central

Register and Start Selling Today

Please have the following before you begin:

- Your business name, address, and contact information
- If your business is VAT registered, your VAT registration details
- A UK or internationally-chargeable credit card with valid billing address
- A phone number where you can be reached during this registration process

Important Notice for International Sellers

If you are registering from a country which is outside of the UK, you will need to read and adhere to the following requirements:

- You will have to provide a bank account in a country supported by Amazon.co.uk in order to be paid. Currently Amazon supports UK, Austrian, French, German and US bank accounts.
- You will be responsible to meet the shipping expectations for all orders you receive.
- Products must be listed in British Pounds and include all taxes.
- All customer facing content and communication must be in English.
- Products that require electric plugs must be supplied with local plugs.
- Please read the following important information for international sellers for more details of your obligations as an international seller.

If you cannot comply with the requirements of this registration, please do NOT continue with this registration process.

Select an Option to Begin

- ⦿ Create a new account (Recommended for Business accounts) **4**
- ○ Use existing Amazon customer account

Sign-In Information

First and Last Name:	
5 **E-mail Address:**	Use an e-mail address that is checked frequently and/or dedicated to business use.
Re-type E-mail Address:	

You are signing up for...

Selling on Amazon - Professional

£ 25.00/mth + per-item seller fees (VAT exclusive)

Fulfilment by Amazon

[Remove]
No Monthly Subscription Fee. Pay per use.

? DID YOU KNOW?
If you find the Pro seller option doesn't work well for your business, you can cancel the service at any time through your seller account page.

HOT TIP: You should create a separate bank account for your Amazon business to keep track of your costs and profits for tax purposes.

Consider Fulfilment by Amazon

With Fulfilment by Amazon (FBA) you send your items to an Amazon facility and they 'pick and pack' them from their warehouse. You are charged a small monthly fee to store your items and also are subject to other handling fees based on the item type and weight. For standard-sized media (books, CDs, software, video games) you'll pay a 'pick and pack' price per unit of £0.50 and a weight-handling fee that varies depending on the item.

- Add FBA to your existing seller account; sell some items through FBA and some through your own business or Amazon seller account.
- Have your items sent with Super Saver Delivery to subscribed Prime members.
- Ship a few or hundreds of items to Amazon's fulfilment centres. You pay based in part on how much storage space you need. There are different fulfilment fees depending on the weight of the product.

? DID YOU KNOW?
Returns for FBA items are handled by Amazon, so you don't have to deal with the shipping or paperwork, though you will want to keep track of the order details for your records.

HOT TIP: Read more about the details of FBA to see if this programme would work for your business. Scroll to the bottom of the main webpage and click on the Fulfilment by Amazon link.

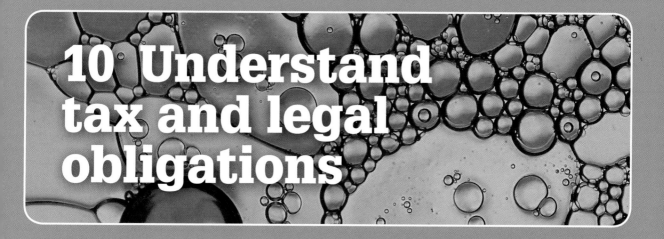

10 Understand tax and legal obligations

Introduction

This chapter looks at the rules and regulations that apply to small business and outlines some steps you need to take, such as deciding on a legal structure for your business and making sure that you are registered to pay your taxes. You'll also learn about some business laws that apply to you. Many of the laws explored here are designed with consumers in mind: keeping them happy by treating them fairly and providing goods and services as described. Following the law can also be good for your business as customers who are treated fairly and have a positive experience with your business are more likely to be return customers. What you'll get in this chapter is a starting point for understanding the legal obligations you have as a small business. You should do more to understand these laws by following the suggested links throughout this chapter.

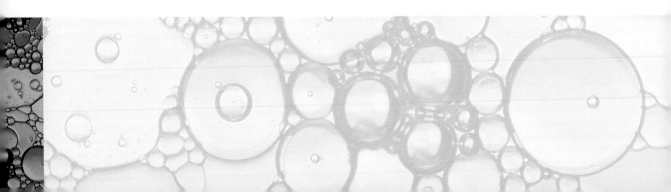

Choose a business structure

The choice you make for your business structure has implications for how much tax you are liable for and what type of records you'll need to keep. If you are an individual starting your own business, you can register as a sole trader, which is the simplest option in terms of reporting and book keeping. If you are working with someone else or have investors, your options will be different. Below are the two most common types of start-up business structures.

- Sole trader: if one person is starting up the business, the individual registers as self-employed with HMRC and files a self-assessment tax return each year. The individual doesn't have to pay any registration fees to work as a sole trader but they are liable for all business debts.

- Partnership: two people in a simple partnership share the business and are both responsible for the business debt. It's not necessary to have a formal agreement but it's usually a good idea to have something in writing. Both partners must register as self-employed.

ALERT: As a sole trader, you are liable for income tax on your profits as well as National Insurance contributions each year.

SEE ALSO: For more help on choosing a business structure and understanding your tax liability, go to www.businesslink.gov.uk/taxhelp

HOT TIP: There are other business types, such as a private limited liability company and statutory business entity, that will be relevant only after you are a more established business or find investors for your business.

Register your business with HMRC

Once you decide on a business model, you need to register your business with HMRC. Each business type will have slightly different registration requirements, but both sole traders and partnerships will register as self-employed. Regardless of whether or not you are liable for VAT, you need to contact HMRC and register so that you can file your annual tax details.

- Register yourself as self-employed for tax purposes within three months of starting your online business.
- Provide your registration details, including your National Insurance number and contact details, to HMRC either via phone or online.
- Keep the Unique Taxpayer Reference (UTR) you receive from HMRC in a safe location in your office or home.

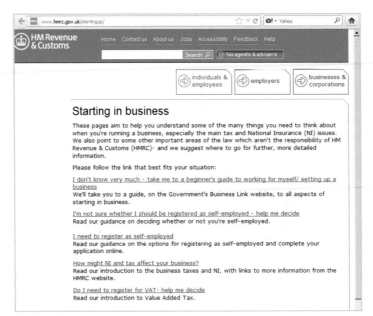

ALERT: If you fail to register your business within three months of starting up, you could be subject to a penalty fine.

DID YOU KNOW?
You have to fill in self-assessment forms for your business earnings even if you have a different day job and work on your business only part-time initially.

Keep clear accounting records

To monitor the health of your business and also to keep clear records for your annual tax filing, get in the habit of establishing a regular record-keeping system as soon as you start up your business. If you register as self-employed, record keeping is relatively straightforward. However, if you set up a different business structure, the requirements for the records you keep will be more stringent. The requirements below are for either self-employed or partnership businesses:

- Record of all sales and takings: bank statements, PayPal statements, invoices that show the income you received from your business.
- Record of all expenses and purchases: all invoices, receipts, cheque stubs and other accounting records related to expenses you incurred as a business.

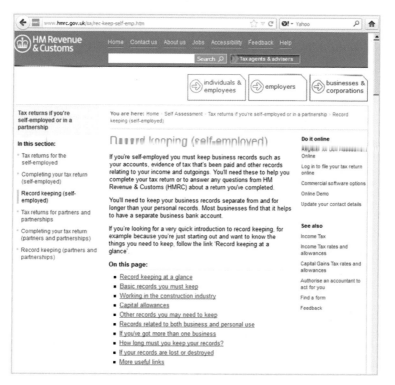

HOT TIP: There are some expenses you can deduct from your annual taxes, including mileage, equipment, professional fees and some household expenses, when working from home.

SEE ALSO: Review the information on the HMRC website about record keeping for self-employed individuals at www.hmrc.gov.uk/rec-keep-self-emp.htm

Consider business insurance

If you work out of your home and use it as an office, your home insurance policy will not cover business equipment such as your computer, printer and copier or any stock you keep in your house to run your business. If any of these items are damaged or stolen, the cost of replacing them could put your start-up business at risk. You can purchase insurance to cover your equipment, premises, stock – or all three.

- Itemise the equipment you use for your business and estimate the combined value.
- List the stock on your premises and its approximate market value.
- Check with your existing insurer to see whether or not they offer a business insurance option and will provide a discount if you add another policy.
- Compare the policies of multiple insurance providers before choosing one.

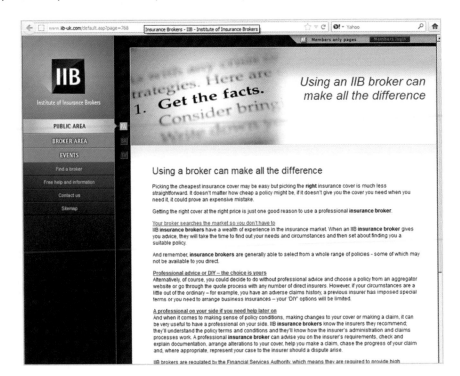

HOT TIP: Go through an insurance broker to get advice on the type of insurance your business might need. You can find a broker at www.iib-uk.com

DID YOU KNOW?
The only type of insurance you are required to have by law is employers' liability insurance if you have employees.

Understand e-commerce regulations

As with other types of commerce, any business you conduct online is subject to a number of different regulations. Most businesses operating online will be subject to E-Commerce Regulations (ECRs) and Distance Selling Regulations (DSRs) and, depending on your business, Provision of Service Regulations (PSRs). These laws are designed to protect consumers who shop online. Below is a basic summary of how the regulations may affect your business – you should take further steps to learn about them. Anyone who sells or advertises goods or services online must comply with the regulations.

- Provide consumers with clear information about your business on your website, including your full contact details, VAT number if you are subject to VAT, clear indication of prices, taxes or postage charges they may incur.

- Outline for customers before they place an order how they can change or cancel an order and when they'll receive an order confirmation.

- Include details of any trade register and the registration number if applicable.

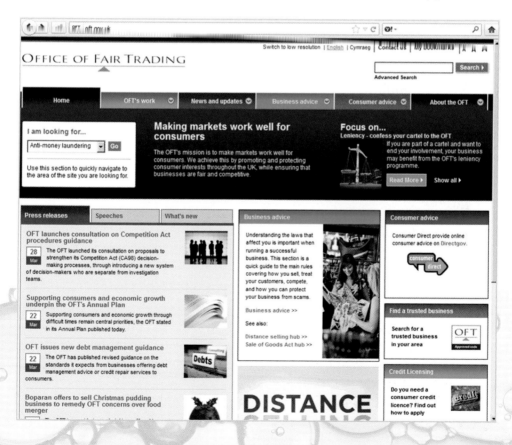

ALERT: Distance trading law allows consumers to cancel and return their order after seven days. There are some exceptions allowed for perishable goods, software that has been opened and flowers, among others.

SEE ALSO: For more information on the laws that apply to your online businesses, go to the Office of Fair Trading website at oft.gov.uk and download more information about the types of regulations outlined above.

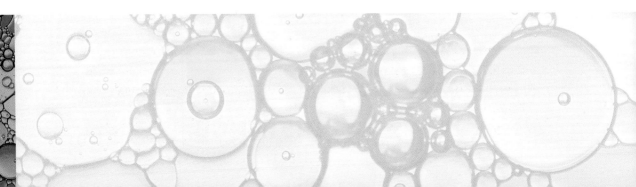
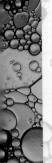

Understand trademarks

A trademark, or brand, distinguishes your products or services as being from your business and distinct from other businesses. Trademarks include a logo, design, phrase or business name that is unique to your business. You need to check that the business name you are operating under, as well as any phrases or slogans you use on your website, are not trademarked. After you check they are unused, you can register your own trademarks to prevent other businesses or individuals from using them.

- Search for trademarks registered at www.ipo.gov.uk/tm/t-find/t-find-text
- Register your trademark with the Intellectual Property Office at www.ipo.gov.uk

ALERT: If you use a trademark that has been registered by another business, even unknowingly, you can legally be prevented from using it.

DID YOU KNOW? Owning a domain name does not confer any trademark protection on your business brand. You must register a trademark to protect your brand.

Understand copyright obligations

Copyright falls under the same jurisdiction of intellectual property law as trademarks, but you don't have to register copyright for any text or images you produce or that you hire others to produce for your business. You should bear in mind the following as they apply to your online business:

- Written and other types of content are automatically protected by copyright law – you don't have to register the text or images on your website.

- Add a copyright symbol © (with your name and year) to your work to let others know that the text or image is protected by copyright laws. You don't have to do this, but it can discourage others from using your work without your permission.

- You can't use other copyrighted sources (e.g. from other businesses or websites) without the permission of the copyright holder.

- Don't sell counterfeit or 'knock-offs' of brand-named goods on your website or anywhere else.

SEE ALSO: For more information on copyright, visit the Intellectual Property Office website at www.ipo.gov.uk/types/copy.htm

ALERT: Copyright applies to a variety of media, including any written work, musical or broadcast work as well as visual or artistic works such as logos, drawings and maps.

Top 10 Online Start-up Problems Solved

Problem 1: The images and layout of my website aren't displaying properly

In some browsers you may find that your website layout is crooked or the images are distorted or hard to make out. Some versions of Internet Explorer can't resize images in GIF file format. If you uploaded a GIF file to your site, this could be the source of the problem. You can change the file format to JPEG to resolve the problem.

1 Open your image-editing software.

2 Open the file you want to change.

3 Click File and select Save As.

4 Select JPEG from the drop-down menu, then click Save.

Save As				×
← →	▾ Style Tees Biz ▾ Sale Item Images	▾ ↻	Search	🔎

File name: Img203

Save as type: JPEG (*.jpg;*.jpeg;*.jpe;*.jfif)

Monochrome Bitmap (*.bmp;*.dib)
16 Color Bitmap (*.bmp;*.dib)
256 Color Bitmap (*.bmp;*.dib)
24-bit Bitmap (*.bmp;*.dib)
JPEG (*.jpg;*.jpeg;*.jpe;*.jfif)
GIF (*.gif)
TIFF (*.tif;*.tiff)
PNG (*.png)

▾ Browse Folders

🔥 **HOT TIP:** You can use Paint or a program that came with your operating system if you don't have a separate image-editing program.

Problem 2: I want to remove the site-builder logo from my website

Most website-building services include their own logo on your website by default. If you are using a free site builder, you probably won't have the option to remove the logo. In Go Daddy, you can remove the logo from your website by doing the following:

1 Go to My Account and launch your Quick Shopping Cart.

2 Click the Set Up menu and select Store Preferences.

3 Untick the box next to Show Powered-By-Quick-Shopping-Cart Badge.

4 Scroll to the bottom of the page and click OK.

5 Click Publish to update your website.

HOT TIP: If you don't have Go Daddy, you should still be able to remove any logos from your website. Look for information in the help section of your website builder or contact customer support for instructions on how to do this.

Problem 3: I want to list a sale item without using a coupon code

If you have stock that has not been terribly successful at the current price, you may want to run a sale on your website to increase the chances of it selling. Rather than offering customers a coupon code, you can reduce the price displayed on the product page. Make sure you let existing customers know about your sale if they have agreed to receive email notifications from you. Do the following from Go Daddy's Quick Shopping Cart:

1 Click Manage and select Products.

2 Click edit on the product you want to put on sale.

3 Scroll down to Prices and click Add New Sales Price.

4 Enter a percentage discount or enter a sales price.

5 Enter a start date and an end date, then click OK.

> **? DID YOU KNOW?**
> The item price will display with a strike through the original price and the new price beneath it.

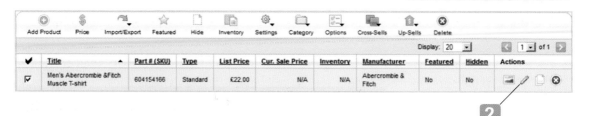

> **! ALERT:** You must click Publish after you make the price changes to your products so that your website updates with the changes.

Problem 4: My website isn't getting hits or is ranking low in the search results

It can take a while for your website to show up in the search results and to attract new visitors. It depends in part on how well optimised your site is and how long your site has been published. If you find that your site isn't listed in the first several pages of the search results with the major search engines, you may need to change your keywords or consider investing in paid search results if you haven't already. Here are some things to bear in mind:

- Experiment with different keywords and expand on your initial list of keywords by getting more ideas from Google AdWords.
- Consider paid advertising with Google or another search engine if you haven't done so already.
- Update and change the content on your site frequently (e.g. make seasonal changes to your page for annual holidays, keep your product images and descriptions up to date or offer an FAQ section).
- Advertise your website offline to targeted audiences. For example, if you sell craft supplies, make sure your website is included in popular craft magazines.
- Create inbound links to your site by connecting with other businesses or individuals. Offer to do the same for them if it makes sense for your business.

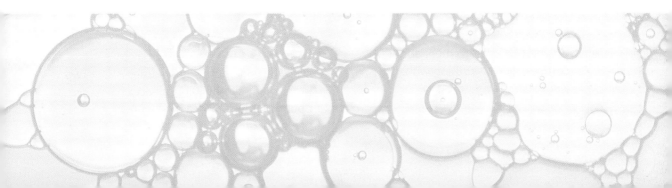

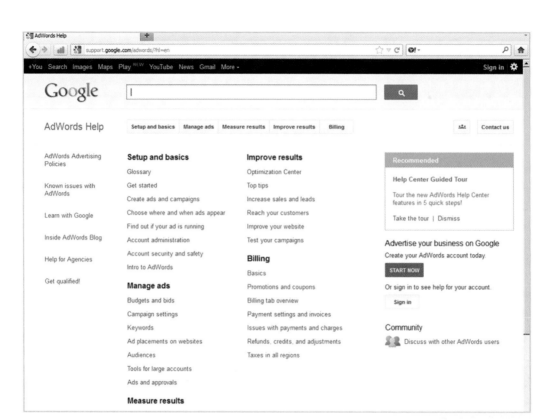

SEE ALSO: Learn more about cost-per-click advertising with Google on its support page: support.google.com/adwords

HOT TIP: A blog is a good way to keep the content of your website fresh. Many site-building services have options for including a blog with your site, sometimes for an extra charge.

Problem 5: How do I link my social media sites to my main website?

If you'd like to advertise the fact that you have a social media website such as Facebook or Twitter, you can usually enable a share option from your site builder. The icons from the social media sites will display on your main page and customers can click on them to 'like' you on Facebook or follow you if you have a Twitter account.

1 Launch your website in Quick Shopping Cart.

2 Click the Set Up menu and select Store Preferences.

3 Scroll down to Social Media and tick Enable Sharing.

4 Tick the box next to the social media site you have.

5 Type your social media site's URL and click OK when you've finished.

6 Update your page.

Social Media ⊙

☑ Enable Sharing **3**

   ☑ Show Facebook account

4   * http://www.facebook.com/ styletees   ⊙

   ☐ Show Twitter account

Preview Options   **5**

☑ Display empty categories during store preview ⊙

OK   Cancel

HOT TIP: If you have a different website builder, check with customer support to see whether or not you can enable this option on your website. Most services have a way to link your main website to any other sites of your choosing.

Problem 6: Can I use my business email in Outlook?

Rather than logging in via your browser each time you want to use your business email, you can link your business email to Outlook on your desktop. The instructions below are for Go Daddy, but other site-builder services have the same option.

1 Log into your account on Go Daddy and scroll down to launch your web email.

2 Click on the Edit icon.

3 Click Start quick setup now.

4 Download the Quick Setup Tool to your computer.

5 Click Run once it's finished downloading and follow the instruction to add it to Outlook.

ALERT: Check you have Outlook on your computer and that you have opened it at least once.

Problem 7: How can I allow customers to pay over the phone?

While you go out of your way to make customers feel comfortable shopping from you, there are some who prefer talking to a person over the phone. You can offer your customers this option by enabling it on your website. They shop and add the item to their cart, select Print and Call, print out the order and call you to arrange payment and shipping. In your Go Daddy Quick Shopping Cart:

1 Launch your website.

2 Click Set Up and select Payment Options.

3 Scroll down to the Print and Call section and click Enable.

4 Add information to the Print and Call set-up such as a phone number or other details.

5 Click OK.

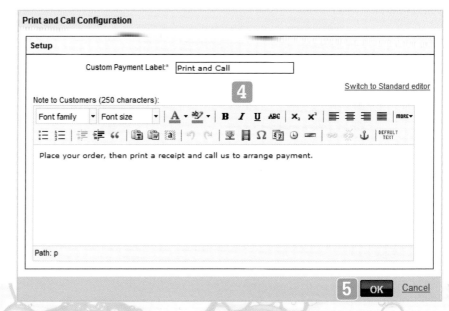

DID YOU KNOW?

PayPal has a secure payment option that customers can use over the phone called Virtual Terminal. You can enter a customer's payment details directly into PayPal.

Problem 8: Can I list products on eBay through my website?

If you have an account on eBay and a Go Daddy Quick Shopping Cart, you can list your products on eBay via your Go Daddy page. Follow the steps below to authorise Quick Shopping Cart eBay Auction Manager:

1 Click on the Promote menu in your Quick Shopping Cart and select eBay Auction Manager.

2 Click Get Started With eBay Now!

3 Sign into eBay with your user ID and password.

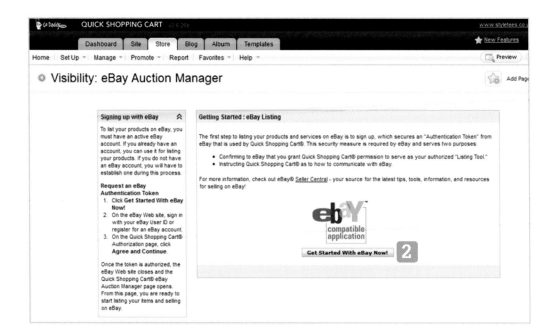

4 Click I agree when prompted by eBay.

5 Click List Item on eBay to get started.

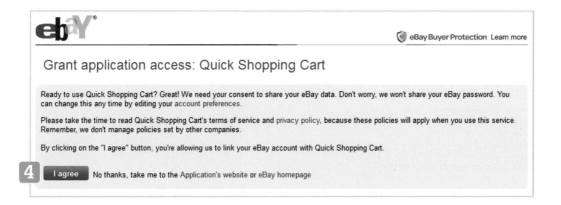

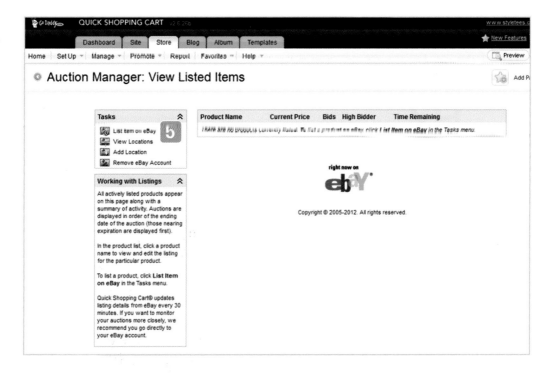

ALERT: It may take a minute or two while the two websites connect. Don't perform any activities in your browser while this process takes place.

Problem 9: How can I protect my business from credit card fraud?

A stolen credit card is easier to use online than in person, which can put small businesses at risk for fraudulent credit card purchases. If a purchase is made that the real cardholder asserts is fraudulent, the full amount of the purchase is sometimes charged back to the business. Do the following to keep your business safe from fraudulent purchases:

- Confirm the name on the card and the card holder address are the same.
- Be wary of very large or unusual purchases and consider contacting any customer who places such an order.
- Check that you have a landline phone number for the customer if you have questions about the order.
- Check whether or not the delivery address has been used before with a different credit card.

! ALERT: Online authorisation of credit cards through your payment provider or merchant bank account confirms only that the card has sufficient funds and that it hasn't recently been reported as stolen. It does not guarantee payment.

▶ SEE ALSO: You can learn about other ways to protect your business from fraud by visiting www.financialfraudaction.org.uk

Problem 10: How do I unpublish my website after I hit Publish on Go Daddy?

If you find a major error on your website after you hit Publish, you can temporarily take your site offline while you fix the problem. The process is called 'parking' your domain name. What visitors see if they type in the URL of your store is a temporary message generated by Go Daddy rather than your home page. To park your domain, log into your account in Go Daddy and do the following:

1 Go to Domains and click Launch.

2 Select the domain name you want to park if you have more than one.

3 Click Set Nameservers.

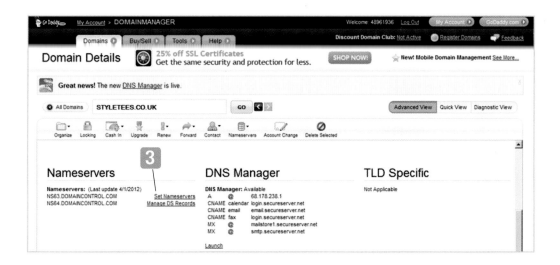

4 Select I want to park my domains.

5 Click OK.

Set Nameservers

If you are hosting your Web site with us (you have a hosting account with us associated with this domain) or you want to Park or Forward your domain, we will automatically set your nameservers for you.

4

○ I want to **park** my domains.

○ I want to **forward** my domains.

○ I have a **hosting account** with these domains.

○ I have **specific nameservers** for my domains.

Did You Know?

Domains using our nameservers benefit from our worldwide DNS presence through Anycast DNS. Learn More

5 OK   Cancel

ALERT: It can take a few hours or more for the change to take effect. Check by typing your site's URL into your browser.